How media and conflicts make migrants

Manchester University Press

How media and conflicts make migrants

Kirsten Forkert, Federico Oliveri,
Gargi Bhattacharyya and Janna Graham

Manchester University Press

Published by Manchester University Press
Altrincham Street, Manchester M1 7JA
www.manchesteruniversitypress.co.uk

British Library Cataloguing-in-Publication Data
A catalogue record for this book is available from the British Library

ISBN 978 1 5261 3811 8 hardback
ISBN 978 1 5261 3813 2 paperback

First published 2020

Typeset
by Toppan Best-set Premedia Limited
Printed in Great Britain
by TJ International Ltd, Padstow

Contents

List of figures

List of figures

Acknowledgements

We wish to thank the participants and co-researchers who have been involved in our project in the UK and Italy. We thank the members of Birmingham Asylum and Refugee Association (BARA), and the Women's Cultural Forum, now known as Global Sistaz United, for sharing their thoughts, insights, experiences and perspectives about global conflicts, legacies of colonialism and the institutionalised cruelty of the immigration system. We thank the Exiled Journalists' Network for their co-operation and participation. We also wish to thank Cantieri Meticci for working with us on the fieldwork in Italy and in developing our findings into theatrical form. We are grateful to Implicated Theatre and, in particular, Amal Khalaf, Aissata Tham and Francis Rifkin for making the UK theatrical production possible and helping us find ways to tell stories otherwise. We also thank Viviana Salvati, as the main author of the Italian script, Francesco Simonetta, as stage director of the 'mise en espace' in Bologna, and Youssef El Gahda, Francesca Falconi, Boubacar Ndia, Jan Nawaz, Abraham Tesfai, as the readers of the 'mise en espace'. We would like to thank Nicholas Vass for his assistance with the 'Alternative Newspaper' workshop images, Olivia Swinscoe for photographing the Birmingham performance and Vika Nightingale for photographing the Nottingham performance. Kirsten would like to thank her colleagues and students at Birmingham City University (BCU) for their support and insights, and the support of the Faculty Research Investment Scheme in writing this book. She also thanks her partner Peter Conlin for being there throughout the project and the writing of the book.

This project would not have been possible without the support of the AHRC's Innovation Award (AH/N008200/1) and so we wish to thank the funder for enabling us to carry out this work. In addition, we thank BCU and the University of East London for their contributions towards the dissemination of this work.

Introduction: conflict, media and displacement in the twenty-first century

When we embarked on the work that informs this book, the term 'refugee crisis' had only recently re-entered European debate. Since that time, considerable energies have been devoted to explaining and critiquing the framing of crisis and the events leading to unprecedented numbers of people in need moving across the globe. This project also reflects on this context where displaced populations meet anti-migrant anxieties, but we have attempted to reframe the discussion to unsettle what has become an increasingly predictable and frozen interchange between irreconcilable points of view.

The book explores how global conflicts are understood as they relate to the European refugee crisis, which has been framed simultaneously as a humanitarian emergency and a security threat. We examine how 'global conflict' has been constructed through media representations, official and popular discourses, and institutional and citizen-led initiatives (such as the many Facebook groups that developed – if only for a brief moment – for hosting refugees and sending donations to refugee camps). We explore how this understanding in turn shapes institutional and popular responses in receiving countries, ranging from hostility – such as the framing of refugees by politicians, as 'economic migrants' who are abusing the asylum system – to solidarity, as in the grassroots citizen initiatives we have mentioned.

The book focuses on the UK and Italy, two countries that have experienced mistrust towards European institutions (intertwined with debates around migration in relation to conflict), connected to disaffection with mainstream politics. Both have faced internal political controversy in response to population movement in the wake of conflict. In both countries, concerns about the role and efficacy of European institutions have converged with debates about borders and sovereignty. In the UK, this is exemplified by the Brexit vote and the mobilisation of xenophobia by the campaign to leave the EU, and in Italy by the anti-asylum and anti-NGO policies of the right-wing coalition government and especially of the Euro-sceptic, far-right former Deputy Prime Minister and Minister of the Interior, Matteo Salvini. Both countries have also seen the development of grassroots refugee solidarity movements, though – as will be seen – these have their limitations.

Our work began with a question about how popular understandings of global conflicts come about. The discussion of Europe's responsibilities to people in movement has resurrected questions about the interdependency of the international community, our responsibilities to each other and the terms of international law. We argue that limited knowledge about the histories and challenges facing different regions of the world – particularly involving the legacy of Western intervention in these countries – leads to an inability to comprehend contemporary global conflicts and also those who have fled those conflicts. In so doing we consider the habits of media use that inform audiences in Italy and the UK, as well as the frameworks of representation utilised by mainstream media to depict global conflict and European interests. We begin from the perspective that the range and manner of contemporary media use is a significant factor in analyses of attitudes to migration, not only in relation to the representation of migrants and migration but also in relation to the larger framing of global interconnectedness and mutual responsibility. In particular, media representations play a central role in popular understandings of global conflicts and other international events. In times of changing global relations and large-scale population movements, what is understood and believed about global events becomes uncertain and, we argue, this uncertainty shapes attitudes to political institutions and to migration.

War and media

Popular understandings of war in recent decades have been refracted through media representations, both the adventures and emotions of war movies and the changing framing of news reporting. Until recently, scholars of international relations and of media studies could feel confident in their identification of the central media accounts of influence. Media institutions could be placed alongside other pillars of power and influence, with overlapping membership and interests charted. We might employ techniques from audience studies to explore the diversity of interpretations in play, but there was a sense of agreement about which text were under consideration.

The emergence of a media landscape far more fragmented, diverse and uncharted than could have been imagined until recently demands a revisiting of this earlier certainty. These matters have remade the study of media (Klinger and Svensson 2014; Noto and Pesce 2018), but have not yet been integrated into the conceptual repertoires of other disciplines. Although we have learned, somewhat slowly, that media representations are of interest to social and political scientists and to those studying international relations and the politics of migration, it is all too clear that we no longer know how audiences put together their media use. Techniques of collating, assembling, sifting and cross-referencing are all developing very rapidly, with studies struggling to keep pace (Pentina and Tarafdar 2014; Schroder 2015; Westlund and Fardigh 2015).

In the field of migration studies, this raises some challenges. The role of the media in creating and sustaining anti-migrant feeling has been a central theme in the field (Szczepanik 2016; Georgiou and Zaborowski 2017). In the UK, the tabloid press, in particular, has been regarded as central to any examination of *xeno-racism* in this country, with this understood as the processes through which 'old racisms' can be redirected towards those made other through their foreignness or alleged foreignness (Sivanandan cited in Fekete 2001). Even the United Nations High Commissioner for Refugees (UNHCR) has rebuked the British press for whipping up hatred against refugees and asylum seekers. Among scholars of racism, it has become accepted that popular media, in particular newspapers, have contributed to a climate of hostility towards migrants of all kinds (Philo, Briant and Donald 2013; Bhatia, Poynting and Tufail 2018). Throughout this project, participants also pointed to the role of the media in encouraging hatred. As we will discuss in relation to the research carried out in the UK, the tabloid press continued to be a cause of concern to migrants, and it was this negative tabloid representation that they sought to challenge. Yet what we learned about news consumption through our survey of media users suggests that emerging news audiences employ a far more flexible and fragmented approach to news coverage. Whatever relentless campaign of demonisation is expressed through the pages of the popular press, this set of meanings may not match the interpretations of media users who increasingly distrust all media sources and, instead, combine multiple sources to construct a composite account of news events.

In response to this changing landscape of media use, and informed by the insights and reminders of our project participants, we have tried to give space to sometimes overlooked debates. These include the impact of Eurocentric modes of understanding global events on the attitudes of media audiences and discussion of the desire of (some) migrants to reposition the events of the twenty-first century in a longer history of colonial relations. These questions, raised repeatedly by participants in the project, lead into the second half of the work: a collective analysis of the institutional processes of 'becoming migrant' and an examination of how scholars and activists might move beyond a fixation on the individual testimony to learn to participate in the co-production of such collective accounts. Later chapters take up each of these themes in more detail.

The representation of international events continues to replicate the representational frameworks of Empire. Mainstream media forms such as film and newspapers perpetuate depictions of most of the world as uncivilised and savage, of a world of victims and saviours, of civilising missions against inexplicable terror, of hordes of needy people who appear out of nowhere. There are few spaces to reflect on the longer histories that bring us here. It is difficult to find any acknowledgement of the histories of dispossession that link North and South and form the background to current conflicts and migratory journeys. As we have learned from the careful analysis of the Glasgow Media Group, news coverage with limited or misleading contextual framing skews the understanding of media audiences (Philo, Briant and Donald 2013). For example, in relation to the struggles for Palestinian rights and self-determination, the preponderance of sympathetic accounts of Israeli priorities, combined with an absence of historical contextualisation, has led British audiences to view Palestinians as the occupiers and Israelis as the occupied.

It is tempting to offer an alternative 'corrected' account of conflicts that acknowledges the impact of imperial histories and regional context. We ended the work on this book with a strong sense that British and Italian audiences needed access to reminders of recent events of significance when reading/watching news about wars. The participants in the research project which served as the basis of this book argued repeatedly for greater engagement with Britain's imperial histories, particularly in relation to countries and regions where populations continued to be displaced by violence. However, we also questioned the idea of 'completing' uneven knowledges. It is true there are glaring gaps in mainstream media accounts of global conflicts. However, these absences cannot be corrected only by adding missing facts. The overall framing of global relations in media and popular accounts shaped by imperial forgetting must be called into question.

As one contribution to this process, in this book we have tried to move away from collecting the sad stories of migrant journeys. We appreciate the power and importance of such narratives, including the political insight and leverage gained from the tactical circulation of such experiential narratives in times of extreme dehumanisation of migrants. However, we also felt uncomfortable with another unquestioning replaying of other people's pain. We recognised the danger of critiquing the weaknesses of mainstream media accounts, including the post-imperial amnesia displayed in relation to global events, and then offering the personal accounts of migrants as a more 'truthful' or 'accurate' version of events. This structure of argument and activity remains closely tied to imperial logics. In particular, the placing of researchers as saviour-translators who can collect and decipher tragic tales, in the process humanising imperial narratives that have lacked this injection of personal experience, seems to misunderstand what is happening and what can happen in the research context. We accept and understand that we cannot 'fix' things. No amount of shared attribution or documenting of voice can make amends for the suffering arising from being deemed irregular.

Instead of proclaiming ourselves as beneficent advocates for the voiceless, we have tried to open the discussion of collective approaches to the development of performance to 'answer back' to the mainstream depiction of migrants, including by offering 'worlded' accounts of history and our global interconnections. Later chapters offer examples of this work.

However, in relation to the representation of migrants, it was not so easy to avoid the demand for positive or better images. In a context of constant vilification in mainstream media and overtly hostile policies from the state, our research participants agreed that there was an urgent need to counter public narratives about migrants and the background to migration. The majority of those we interviewed for this book were or had been in the asylum process. However, a significant proportion came from countries from which migrants entered through a number of routes, not necessarily asylum (regardless of the role of political unrest and violence in shaping migratory choices) but also as workers, students or through some other means – but then, through various personal and political circumstances, found themselves on the wrong side of the immigration system.

The recurring complaint was not that the authorities refused to recognise the veracity and urgency of any individual claim, although this urgency was there. Instead, what emerged in discussion was a larger critique of the strategic role of Western know-nothingness. The repeated demeaning representations of migrants, including the almost open incitement to hatred, relied on the silencing of histories of colonial exploitation, resource-grabbing and earlier border-crossing. This silencing of imperial pasts limited what could be communicated or understood in relation to contemporary conflicts and served to absolve European audiences of a sense of connection and responsibility to other parts of the world. This, in turn, undermined individual claims by confirming a view of global relations consisting of a put-upon affluent North and a desperate and needy South.

Being made into migrants by the state

This topic is a central theme throughout the book. The active limitations that are placed on the lives of 'migrants' in the name of sovereignty and border control have been well-documented. However, there are other less formal 'demands' that arise with the status of migrant, and contradictory pressures that are placed on them. Migrants, if vulnerable, must not plan ahead or plan to travel or plan to return – because they must demonstrate constantly that they are building roots here (at the same time as immigration restrictions make it difficult for people to live a settled existence). Migrants must not be too resilient, because this can damage their application for regularised status (which, in the case of asylum claims, is based on demonstrating suffering and need). Migrants must show that they make a contribution, but the contribution must not be too competent or too lucrative or too highly qualified or too unskilled lest they be accused of stealing jobs from locals. Most of all, migrants must not take their attention for a moment from their precarious immigration status. To do so is to potentially destabilise their claim, literal and metaphorical, to gain a place of stability.

In our interviews and workshops held in London, Birmingham, Nottingham, Pisa and Bologna as part of the research project which served the basis of this book, we asked asylum seekers and refugees to critically reflect on how they have been constructed as migrants in their encounters with the state, public institutions and with members of society. Our participants interpreted this primarily in two ways. The first, which was the most obvious, was about the formal conditions of their immigration status, which both in the UK and in Italy are extremely restrictive. Asylum seekers in the UK, for example, are not allowed to work; those who have been in the country for 12 months awaiting a decision are able to seek work, but can only access jobs on the shortage list, which on a practical level is impossible to many (Fletcher 2008). They rely on benefits currently totalling £37.75/week (less for those whose claims have been refused), which are significantly less than for those on Jobseeker's Allowance. They are housed in temporary accommodation which is managed by G4S, a global private security firm with a history of controversy around human rights abuses. In Italy, asylum seekers are allowed to work after two months, although their residency permit cannot be converted into a work permit. However, in practice they face difficulties accessing the regular labour market being therefore highly vulnerable to exploitation (Filiera Sporca 2016). Moreover, since 2018, asylum seekers face obstacles in registering to municipal registry office, and they no longer have access to language courses and training. They are housed in reception centres, some of which are in remote locations, making it difficult to find work and integrate into society. Being a migrant, for our participants, was about the strictly circumscribed existence of living under such restrictions, which one of our participants revealingly characterised as 'life in handcuffs'. Overall, our work seeks to understand the multiple practices that construct this cage of constraint and to understand the connections between these constraining processes and our understandings of war and international law.

About the research which produced this book

The book arises from the AHRC-funded research project entitled *Conflict, memory, displacement*. We discuss the findings of our research in detail throughout the book. However, we will briefly set out the key findings from our project here:

1. **The mainstream media only covers some of the conflicts in the world.** Several conflicts and regions (such as Eritrea or Colombia) receive almost no coverage, or only in relation to people seeking asylum. When there is coverage, there is no context given for the conflicts – news coverage tends to be about day-by-day military operations, 'terrorist' incidents or individual examples of suffering, but little about the history or geopolitics of the region, or the causes of the conflicts.
2. **Mainstream media coverage of conflicts is generally filtered through an idea of 'Western interests'.** The notion of 'Western interests' may vary according to the situation, including the involvement of 'our troops' on the ground, the kidnapping or killing of fellow citizens, the impact on 'our national security', 'our economy', 'our access to natural/energy resources', etc. In recent years conflicts, in particular in Syria, have been represented as of interest to Western audiences because they result in 'mass migrations' towards Europe, producing the so-called 'refugee crisis'.
3. **Where direct Western intervention has been a central factor (Afghanistan, Iraq, Libya), mainstream media have often presented conflicts as resulting from the**

failures of 'great men'. In the UK much coverage of the Iraq War returns to the allegedly flawed character of Tony Blair and his personal responsibility for the military intervention. A similar interpretation occurs also in the coverage of Libya, in relation to his rapidly changing relations with the country and its former leader Gaddafi. In Italy, this focus on the flawed personalities of 'great men' also overshadows any other deeper explanation of ongoing wars.

4. **Mainstream media coverage offers almost no route to understanding histories of Empire, i.e. colonialism and neo-colonialism, as a factor in contemporary conflicts and the management of human displacement.** In addition, asylum seekers and refugees feel that British and Italian populations know little about their countries, in general, and about the histories of Empire in particular. They also argue that this absence of knowledge hampers their understanding of the causes of contemporary migration and also reinforces the sense of Western entitlement.
5. **While mainstream media sources are still frequently consulted, people are increasingly looking to alternative news sources in order to understand global conflicts, including social media and news comedy programmes.** Consumption of news media has been undergoing a process of rapid change, with traditional media being supplemented with social media and other sources (Gordon, Rowinski and Stewart 2013; AGCOM 2018). Our interest is in how these changes might enable different narratives about conflict and migration, or alternatively, perpetuate new forms of xenophobia and racism.

In the UK and Italy, the young people we surveyed as part of our research expressed suspicion of the media and its 'hidden agendas', due to media ownership, and/or political interference. In Italy, the suspicion extended to online content, because of the perceived widespread use of 'fake news' and the fear of manipulative practices such as clickbait. In general, people chose to consult a range of news in order to piece together accounts that could be verified by multiple sources. In the UK, people use alternative media to 'check' international news, especially from countries that they know or to which they are connected.

6. **Global and national institutions are increasingly seen to be ineffective in the resolution of conflicts and the management of displacement, which produces radical distrust.** In the UK, Eurosceptic mainstream media coverage framed European and British foreign aid as supporting corrupt regimes and conning the British taxpayer. In the Italian mainstream media, the main targets of criticism included EU institutions, who are accused of 'leaving Italy alone' in the face of unprecedented numbers of arrivals by sea between 2014 and 2016. This radical distrust was also present in the initiatives studied in our online ethnography. In the UK and in Italy, for those with strong anti-immigration views, this radical distrust can be filtered through a conspiratorial frame in which immigrants, particularly Muslims, are seen to threaten social cohesion, and governments who let them in as either deliberately or unwittingly facilitating social breakdown. In Italy, popular distrust has extended to NGOs engaged in search and rescue operations in the Central Mediterranean, who are suspected of colluding with organised crime networks.

7. **Refugees and their supporters make use of social media platforms to organise mutual aid, in the absence of state support and official hostility.** In the UK and Italy, local populations who want to help refugees will engage in mutual aid practices (such as donating necessities or raising money for charities) in the absence of lack of state support but also to counter perceptions of British or Italian society as uncaring and intolerant. Refugees themselves also use social media platforms for sharing information and mutual support in the face of an immigration system which seems

cruel and impenetrable, and in the absence of safe and legal means to travel.

8. **Migrants are stereotyped as tellers of sad stories by the media, the government and the voluntary sector.** Both media and the immigration process demand that people present themselves as 'deserving victims' and that they share stories of personal pain. Migrants recognise this but also question the benefits to them of repeatedly retelling their stories to every audience – and migrants are concerned about what will be done with their stories (including by researchers). At the same time, the participants in the UK were unwilling to identify times they have had fun, due to the fear that this could be used to undermine their claim to be 'deserving'. In effect, this expectation forces those seeking status to constantly retell their 'story' in order to 'prove' their case to every person they meet.

   In Italy, respondents expressed the feeling of being under suspicion of lying in order to receive protection. This was also reflected in media coverage which stressed the need to distinguish between 'refugees' and 'economic migrants' (often stigmatised as 'illegal aliens'), or showed suspicion towards those who were fleeing persecution, but did not come from countries at war.

9. **People are 'made into migrants' by the government, the media and members of society.** By this we mean that the category of 'migrant' is constructed actively as a means of erasing other identities and as a process of creating a new social identity that is demeaned and constrained by official processes. A sense of being 'other', illegitimate and undeserving lie at the core of this identity.

10. **There is a blur between being 'made a migrant' and racialisation – and even being a 'model immigrant' is no protection against this.** However, although many respondents spoke of facing racism on the grounds of how they looked, they also described additional or distinct experiences

as a result of their immigration status. In our initial view, the processes of migrantification and racialisation reinforce each other at key moments, but remain distinct.

11. **Faith, music, comedy, self-organisation and knowledge of history (including legacies of colonialism and anti-colonial struggles) can be important resources in challenging injustice and dehumanisation.** These resources both undo migrantification, by forwarding different ways of being, and provide a politicised critique of Eurocentrism and the limited knowledge within Western society of other parts of the world.

Researching conflict, media and displacement

In undertaking this research, we bring together important recent debates in media and cultural studies about media use and the status of 'news' media in the articulation of popular consciousness, with central questions from migration studies concerning popular responses to global events and the displacement of people. We argue that there is a need for a critical appraisal of audience interaction with news media and how this impacts our understanding of population movement.

This research also represents an attempt to learn from the analytic insights of those who have been displaced. A range of engaged scholarship has focused, understandably, on reinserting the voices of migrants, refugees and asylum seekers into public accounts of movement and the impacts of bordering. However, we wished to avoid making yet another request for personal testimony, not least due to the parallels between state bordering practices that demanded repeated performances of painful life stories as evidence of entitlement to entry. Instead, we tried to organise our discussions with migrant participants around terms of shared analysis, taking guidance from those who had been made into 'migrants' in shaping our discussion of attitudes to world events and population movement.

In order to explore these interconnected questions, we carried out the following fieldwork:

- Media analysis of two UK and three Italian newspapers covering a selection of countries experiencing conflicts and people seeking protection, including some which have been largely visible in the media (such as Afghanistan, Iraq, Syria and Libya), and others which have received less attention despite still experiencing conflicts and sending many asylum seekers (such as Eritrea and Somalia).
- A survey of over 200 people aged 18–33 in the UK and Italy about how they use the media and how this use helps them understand global conflicts, displacement and the role of political institutions.
- Online ethnography of citizen solidarity initiatives (including Facebook groups for addressing refugees' basic needs, hosting refugees in private homes, and crowdfunder pages) and anti-refugee or anti-migrant groups.
- Semi-structured interviews with over 30 asylum seekers and refugees in the UK and Italy, where they were asked to critically reflect on their experiences within the asylum system and in the receiving countries, and the political situation in their country of origin. Our interest was in the construction of 'migrant' as a new identity, one that appeared to override all other aspects of identity. These interviews were constructed to avoid requests for sad stories and we tried to convey our different focus to those we interviewed.
- Workshops in which material from media analyses and interviews was shared in order to encourage critical reflections about the asylum process, encounters with non-migrant populations, memories of conflicts in their country of origin and the impact of bordering processes on everyday life. From these workshops, our participants devised two theatrical performances, one in Italy and one in the UK and created an exhibition of an imagined

alternative newspaper called *The Double Standard* which spoofed mainstream media from a migrant perspective. We also created visualisations of key ideas relating to the process of being made into a 'migrant'. The visualisations and the spoof newspaper have been reproduced in the third and fourth interludes, and can also be accessed online at conflictmemorydisplacement.com.

The structure of the book

In our opening chapter we consider media accounts of the 'European refugee crisis', including the construction of crisis as a threat to Europe. This chapter builds on our analysis of mainstream media in Italy and Britain and the manner in which issues of international politics, war and population movement are presented and framed in news accounts. In particular, we consider the role of mainstream media in creating a concerted amnesia around Europe's history in relation to other parts of the world, a syndrome that we refer to as 'postcolonial innocence'.

In the second chapter we revisit questions about the representation of war and conflict and the impact of these representations on popular understandings of war. We frame this discussion in relation to changes in the theorisation of war and of global politics. By discussing these matters with media users in Italy and Britain,[1] this chapter points to the uncertainty and uneven knowledge of the world that is inculcated by mainstream media platforms.

The third chapter follows on from this consideration of mainstream media to think about the utilisation of alternative media, including by migrants and by those seeking to build solidarity with migrants. We include here a discussion of how migrants use social media as a method of retaining a connection with their home country and also with other migrants. Alongside this, this chapter outlines the use of social media as a platform through which to organise solidarity actions and to create new spaces of political affinity. We also explore how social media platforms have been used by anti-immigrant groups.

Chapter 4 considers in greater detail the manner in which people in movement are transformed into 'migrants'. This includes consideration of the manner in which official processes, structured to marginalise and, apparently, stigmatise migrants, work alongside popular antagonism to migrants and the everyday racisms embedded in Italian and British society.

The final chapter returns to the demands for performance placed on people in movement. Our project included collaborative work with theatre practitioners and workshops with participants where questions of 'migrantification' were used to devise performances. Here we critique the continuing demand that migrants tell their 'sad stories' and consider the tactics that can emerge from thinking about performance critically and imaginatively.

Between chapters, we include brief pieces that exemplify key moments of the project and the voices and thoughts of our participants. Our research gathered this other kind of material as an alternative to the first-person narrative of migration/displacement that is so easy to objectify. Jokes, songs, tableaux and alternative readings of mainstream media, on the other hand, place individual voices in networks of shared meaning and (sometimes) laughter. Much of this laughter was the dark laughter of dark times, but it is still a laughter that unsettles the disciplinary demands of proving your 'status'. The interludes give the reader a flavour of this other mode of talking about and to each other. Other visual outcomes of the project can be seen at www.conflictmemorydisplacement.com.

Why analyse media in an era of distrust?

The power of the media is under question in our time. Not the reach or the ubiquity or the manner in which popular consciousness is mediatised, but the sense that media organisations can present messages that are received in any form of coherence by audiences. Audiences have learned that mainstream media outlets can be considered as extensions of the elite, and, in times of disaffection with the state or with the power of elites, media messages can be challenged or ridiculed.

In the chapters that follow, we offer an initial account of the interplay between a world of diversifying but distrustful media use, uncertainty about the shape of global politics and the impact of these overlapping and highly partial understandings on those who are displaced by conflict. If we have an over-arching point it is this: not only the world itself but also how people learn about the world is changing rapidly. Understanding attitudes to migrants and other apparently 'local' political concerns demands a step back to consider this unstable global context of (mis)understanding. Together we hope that these modes of analysis and discussion offer a different framing of some key questions of our time. As we stumble towards (or away from) some new or renewed understanding of international responsibility, these questions of popular understandings through media use and the impact of such popular understandings on our relations to each other demand attention.

Notes

1 Translations of survey answers, interviews and media sources from Italian to English are provided by Federico Oliveri.

1

How postcolonial innocence and white amnesia shape our understanding of global conflicts

Introduction

In this chapter, we examine the main narratives used to make sense of the so-called 'European migration crisis' and the relationship to global conflicts. Through the powerful yet highly questionable 'crisis' frame (De Genova 2016a), certain events have received international news coverage and play an important role within common-sense visions of 'reality', whilst others have been largely ignored. Bearing in mind the available cross-European media coverage analyses of the migration crisis (Berry et al. 2016; Chouliaraki, Georgiou and Zaborowki 2017), we focus on the narratives which shape the way British and Italian news media and public discourses interpret population movement in relation to wars and violent conflict from 2014 to 2016. We also explore how these narratives perpetuate distrust of national and European institutions, undermine solidarity and empathy, and strengthen popular support for populist legal reforms aimed at undermining the right of asylum, and the rights of migrants in general.

We argue that the mediatisation of global conflicts and the 'European migration crisis' has been primarily constructed around the self-interests of 'receiving countries', and this undermines any serious effort to grasp the socio-economic and political contexts of people's decision to leave. In this chapter, we discuss how Italian and British media have covered global conflicts and how the movement of people is presented when they flee these conflicts. We explore how narratives of global conflicts are shaped by the forgetting of Western responsibilities for old and new colonialism, including military interventions abroad and militarised border controls. We are examining these narratives as a postcolonial discourse produced by 'receiving countries' about themselves and 'the others' crossing their borders.

Questioning the 'crisis' frame

Refugee crisis. Migrant crisis. Humanitarian crisis. Solidarity crisis. EU governance crisis. Crisis of European values and principles. Crisis of humanity. Crisis of asylum law. There has been a proliferation of crisis discourses in the media and in public discourses, aiming to make sense of recent mass movements of people arriving from the Middle East, Asia and Africa to Europe. Our aim is to deconstruct this widespread and often unquestioned use of a 'crisis' frame, arguing that the autonomous free movement of non-European people confronts us with a border crisis (Vaughan-Williams 2015; De Genova 2016a) and a racial crisis (De Genova 2016b). This puts into question the current political construction of Europe and, more generally, the current global border regime based on differential mobility rights (Oliveri 2017). From this perspective:

> The 'crisis' of border control and 'migration management' may [...] be seen to be a crisis of state sovereignty that is repeatedly instigated, first and foremost, by diverse manifestations of the autonomous subjectivity of human mobility itself. (De Genova 2016a)

Thinking of a situation as a crisis creates a vicious cycle, whereby the very definition of a situation as a crisis puts in motion the 'catastrophisation' of events (Ophir 2010). This catastrophisation legitimises exceptional measures, including the use of force, over established practices or the rule of law. The human suffering eventually caused by these states of exception produces new emergency conditions (a crisis within the crisis), requiring further exceptional measures. In the case of the 'European migration crisis', the subversive effects of human mobility have served as a justification for the re-bordering of territories and societies across the Euro-Mediterranean space. For instance, Central and Central-Eastern European states closed and militarised their borders in order to close the Balkan route after the 'long summer of migration' in 2015. After the terrorist attack in Paris in November 2015, fears about a large influx of people seeking protection provoked several European countries to suspend the Schengen Convention on the abolition of internal border controls. In the case of the French-Italian border (as discussed in chapter 3) this arrangement lasted much longer and extended further than the temporary suspensions normally allowed by the Schengen Borders Code.

The Hotspot approach,[1] the EU-Turkey agreement and further plans for externalising asylum procedures to countries outside of Europe have been put into place since 2015 to reinforce the European border regime. For example, EU leaders have discussed co-operation on development policies serving the purpose of preventing migration, such as, for example, in the case of Niger, a country crossed by migratory routes from Western and Central Africa towards Libya and the Mediterranean Sea. Niger has been the primary beneficiary of the EU Emergency for Africa Trust Fund, launched after the 2015 Valletta Summit in order to finance projects aimed at eradicating the root causes of migration directly in African countries, but also at co-operation with border authorities in order to prevent people from travelling to Libya. In Summer 2018 the EU leaders adopted the strategic concept of 'regional disembarkation platforms': reception centres in North Africa aimed to provide rapid processing of asylum claims, and to distinguish between economic migrants and those in need of international protection. This approach had the officially stated aim of '[reducing] the incentive to embark on perilous journeys' (European Commission 2018). In September

2015 EU states committed to relocating up to 160,000 asylum seekers from Italy and Greece to other countries within two years, later revising the figure down to 98,000: 39,600 from Italy. Only asylum seekers from countries such as Syria, Eritrea and Somalia, for which the recognition rate at EU level is 75% or higher, were in fact eligible for relocation. Only 9,078 applicants had been relocated by the end of the relocation programme on 27 September 2017, while by 30 October 2018 12,700 had been relocated. This demonstrates how efforts to relocate asylum seekers or refugees across EU members states have essentially failed.

In this way, official political and media discourses have operationalised the language and tactics of crisis:

> What is fundamentally a moment of governmental impasse – in short, a 'crisis' of territorially – defined state power over transnational, cross-border human mobility – has been mobilised and strategically deployed as 'crisis' for the reconfiguration of tactics and techniques of border policing and immigration and asylum law enforcement. (De Genova 2016a)

These crisis discourses normalised the narrative of a low–medium intensity conflict against unwanted and uncontrolled human mobility. Common-sense, twentieth-century understandings of global conflict are of limited use in grappling with the complexities of 'new wars' (Kaldor 2012). This might partly explain the ambiguity of European public opinion towards shipwrecks in the Mediterranean, ranging from official compassion to indifference or even satisfaction at migrant deaths, as has been expressed in Italian news media and on social media. Ultimately, if migrants are constructed as the enemies, their lives are not 'grievable' (Butler 2009).

Crisis discourses also give the impression that events take place within a very narrow timeframe, making it more difficult to situate them within longer historical continuities; with 'always-on' digital media, this question of temporality becomes even more pronounced. The dominant narrative of the 'refugee crisis' presents the crisis as beginning as the spring of 2015, peaking in autumn of 2015 and then subsiding in 2016 with the closure of the Balkan route and the implementation of the EU-Turkey deal. However, examining migration trends across Italy challenges this narrative of the 'European migration crisis' as primarily a Central and Northern-European phenomenon affecting wealthy Western European nations during and after 2015. In reality, semi-peripheral and peripheral European states such as Italy have already experienced significant flows at least since the aftermath of the 2011 Arab Revolutions. In October 2013 many Syrian families and single parents with children began to arrive in Milan and set up camp in the city's busy rail hub, with the camp growing by the day as charities and city officials tried to assist those travelling to other European countries.

Postcolonial representations of Europe and its 'others'

Narratives framing the situation as a 'crisis' which only began in 2015 and only affects wealthy European countries reflects a particular blindness around longer legacies of conflict and violence, and particularly those resulting from colonial oppression. In exploring this legacy, we are drawing on concepts of white amnesia (Hesse 1997) and postcolonial innocence to grasp the deeper political dimensions underlying the mediation of the 'European refugee crisis'. In doing so, we stress the lack of will or capacity by former colonisers to recognise how longer histories of colonialism shape contemporary global politics including global inequalities, violent conflicts, conflict-related migration and border controls. Receiving countries do not accept responsibility in relation to the reasons why people flee their countries, or for their deaths at the border: both circumstances are 'depoliticised' as natural events (Oliveri 2016). Instead, others are held responsible: for example, in Italy border deaths have been attributed to human traffickers and even to NGOs engaged in search and rescue operations in the

Mediterranean (the latter being seen as implicated within organised crime, to be discussed below).

If European nations are not seen to bear any responsibility for global conflicts, this reinforces their perceived role as global peacekeepers who play a largely benign role within foreign interventions. Wars taking place outside the West are perceived as the result of atavistic religious or ethnic conflicts and as intrinsic to racialised communities in non-Western countries. In the most paranoid versions of this logic, migrants threaten to import the 'barbaric' world-views into Western cultures, provoking social conflict.

Raising the question of responsibility is not only about recognising, as Ida Danewid points out in 'White Innocence and the Black Mediterranean', that:

> the majority of migrants seeking asylum in Europe are coming from countries that until recently were under colonial rule. Libya and Eritrea were Italian colonies until 1947; Somalia was ruled by Italy and Britain until 1960; Syria was a French protectorate under the Mandate System until 1946; Britain invaded and occupied Afghanistan three times until formal independence in 1919. (Danewid 2017: 1680)

More radically, it is about recognising that the majority of 'refugee-producing countries' have been the target of Western armed interventions or political interference during the post-Cold War era: for example, Afghanistan, Iraq, Syria, South Sudan and Somalia (UNHCR 2018).

In considering the 'crisis' framing within postcolonial terms it is important to bear in mind the differences between the colonial and imperial histories of the UK and Italy, not only in terms of specific practices of colonisation during the last two centuries, but also in terms of diverging processes of decolonisation, different immigration paths from former colonies and uneven consciousness of their colonial past. It is also important to understand the prefix 'post' followed by 'colonialism' in terms of an ongoing, yet systematically denied or forgotten, continuity in the domination of Western powers on the rest of the world, despite the decolonisation and formal independence of former colonial states.

The concept of 'white amnesia', developed by Barnor Hesse in 'White Governmentality' (1997), helps to understand how the perceived threat of racialised outsiders connects with the forgetting of colonial legacies (Calchi Novati 2008) and the careful denial of any eventual 'guilty conscience' for the consequences of colonialism. The legacies of exploitation, oppression and violence, which continue to mark former colonies and world politics, are not considered or worked through:

> 'whiteness' refers not only to the occlusion of its racialized history, but also to its resistance to questioning as a racialized identity, particularly where it insinuates and conceals itself discursively as the horizon of universal representation. It is a 'white mythology' which 'has erased within itself the fabulous scene that has produced it, the scene that nevertheless remains active and stirring, inscribed in white ink, an invisible design covered over in the palimpsest' (Derrida 1982: 213). This hegemonic structure of 'whiteness' forgets its contested antecedents, it forgets what 'others' remember; in effect this 'white amnesia' represses the historical context of racism because the threat of the 'racialized other' absorbs all attention. (Hesse 1997: 86)

Amnesia involves the resisting of self-questioning, particularly around whiteness as universal representation against which racialised outsiders are defined and treated as objects of fear. Whiteness, for instance, as Gloria Wekker characterises it, is 'so ordinary, so lacking in characteristics, so normal, so devoid of meaning' (2016: 2) while racialised identities become politically and emotionally loaded.

White amnesia also has similarities with how Paul Gilroy has theorised postcolonial melancholia, as a 'depressed reaction that inhibited any capacity for responsible reconstructive practice' (2004: 107). Postcolonial melancholia is frequently expressed through fears about the loss of identity and culture, in relation to a perceived golden era of social cohesion before mass immigration (discounting historical experiences of racism or even fascism – this is where the neutrality of 'whiteness' is significant); it also involves nostalgia for a lost era of imperial dominance in which Britain's and Italy's role was perceived as largely benevolent (Del Boca 1984). For instance, nostalgia for Empire was quite apparent in the UK during the 2016 campaign to leave the EU, as various politicians pitted the EU against the Commonwealth association of former British colonies (the connections with the history of Empire were not seen to be controversial), and rhetoric about restoring a previous imperial greatness was common (Martill 2017). The forms of forgetting or denying of colonial power, that 'the others' remember and still experience, will be explored here.

White amnesia also plays a significant role in Italy's denial or underplaying of its fascist, racist and colonial past, as well as the key role played by 'race' and 'colonial fractures' in nation-building and the so-called 'Southern Question' (Mellino 2012). In particular, the myth of the 'intrinsically decent character' of the Italian people is based in historical amnesia around the violent acts perpetrated by the Italian army against the colonised populations in Ethiopia and Libya. According to the historian Angelo Del Boca, this has been a deliberate attempt by the Italian government to rehabilitate the national self-image in the aftermath of fascism, and during the decade following decolonisation (Del Boca 2005). The fact that decolonisation was a largely peaceful process following the World War II peace agreement lent credibility to this positive image of Italy. Moreover, the fact that Italy did not receive significant numbers of immigrants from the former colonies after decolonisation corroborated its self-perception as a white, homogeneous nation with no responsibilities in relation to long-term African impoverishment and lack of autonomous and stable economic development, and therefore for some of the root causes for migration flows.This lack of a critical engagement with the past and persistent nostalgic attachment to colonial values (Del Boca 1984) provides the cultural background for a paternalistic, yet restrictive approach to immigration. This background may also explain the self-representation of

Italy as a 'welcoming country' free of racism which 'lost its patience', overwhelmed by 'uncontrolled migration' and by too many 'illegal aliens', left alone by the EU and by other EU countries in dealing with this 'invasion'.

In addition to drawing on these theorisations of white amnesia, we are also developing the concept of 'postcolonial innocence' in order to explain Western anxieties about the movement of non-Western people escaping from lives made unsustainable. Although related, we mean this in a slightly different way from Anna Hartnell's critique of moral superiority within postcolonial studies (2010: 452). For us, postcolonial innocence involves a disavowal of responsibility for the legacies of colonisation and how these shape global inequalities and present-day global conflicts. The disavowal of this responsibility leads Western nations to perceive their role within global conflicts as essentially benign (for example as global peacekeepers and builders of democracy within civilising missions), without considering their role in creating the conditions which produce poverty and violence.

Another aspect of postcolonial innocence (as it is underpinned by this disavowal of responsibility) is Western nations' self-perception as essentially benevolent and generous to people on the move, and the belief that any support to refugees is an offer of humanitarian goodwill. This narrative is common within anti-immigrant rhetoric which presents immigrants as ungrateful recipients or even as abusers of this generosity. This will be discussed in relation to the media coverage of search-and-rescue operations in the Mediterranean and the hardening of public opinion in Italy against immigrants.

White amnesia and postcolonial innocence in the British and Italian media

How do these dynamics play out in UK and Italian media framing of the 'European migration crisis', and the conflicts which fed this crisis? One way in which white amnesia and postcolonial innocence are manifested is through the general inability to recognise current wars or situations of political violence as part of a longer history of old and new colonialism in which Western nations bear responsibility. This is evident in our sample of selected British and Italian newspaper coverage of Afghanistan, Iraq, Somalia and Eritrea, using the *Guardian* and *Daily Mail* in the UK and *La Stampa*, *La Repubblica* and *Corriere della Sera* in Italy. These newspapers were chosen due to their profile in the country and to represent differing editorial voices and politics. However, despite the very obvious differences in the coverage of migrants, it seemed to us that newspapers from different points in the political spectrum represented global conflict in very similar terms. Most notably, all of them failed to cover any conflict in terms other than the implications for European political and economic interests.

The articles were identified on Nexis using the terms 'Name of country + war OR bombing OR troops OR ceasefire OR peace talks OR war crimes OR civilians OR international OR terrorism OR civil war or human rights OR crime OR drugs' and the equivalent in Italian. The timeframe included: 28 December 2014–28 January 2015 to coincide with the NATO withdrawal from Afghanistan; 30 September 2015–30 October 2015 to coincide with the Russian bombing of Syria; and 6 July 2016–6 August 2016 to coincide with the release of the findings of the Chilcot Inquiry. We quickly found that this approach made it impossible to consider representations of a number of longstanding conflicts. For ongoing conflicts (such as Eritrea), we mapped newspaper coverage over a two-year period (2014–16). We then examined the construction of the conflict in each article: actors, causes, proposed solutions, and so on, but also who was being quoted. We looked at whether or not local populations were quoted and the type of commentary they were asked to provide.

Although, in the UK, there was generally more analysis of the geopolitical context of conflicts in the *Guardian* than in the *Daily Mail*, overall there was little in-depth discussion about why particular violent conflicts take place. Instead, news articles on Afghanistan and Iraq focused primarily on individual military operations (in some cases framed in terms of 'our troops in the field', common in the *Daily Mail*), isolated terrorist incidents and undetermined human casualties. When local residents in those regions were quoted it was often as eyewitnesses of tragic incidents, but they were rarely asked for their opinions about causes and dynamics of the conflicts, or their views on how the conflicts could be resolved.

Where Western military intervention was a major factor – such as for example in Afghanistan and Iraq – conflicts were presented as the 'failings of great men' or the strategic failures of military organisations, causing ordinary people to lose their lives. For example, the Chilcot Inquiry (published on 6 July 2016) was part of the sample. Much UK coverage returned to the allegedly flawed character of Tony Blair, his ego and his willingness to please the US, resulting in personal responsibility for the situation in Iraq, but also in relation to changing relations with Libya. In fact, in 2015 the Blair government came under scrutiny for collusion with the regime in Libya and close relations with former leader Muammar Gaddafi, particularly in the wake of revelations that the regime was using violence and torture towards opponents of the regime (Cobain 2015). Global history was framed as a matter for individual global leaders, driven by their personal characteristics and relationships with other global leaders, leaving deeper questions about economic or geo-political interests in the regions out of the discussion.

Overall, there was a sense of conflicts being filtered through 'Western interests'. For example, Syria in particular has been represented as of interest to Western audiences because these conflicts may result in refugees entering Europe. This obscures the fact that the majority of Syrian refugees, in fact, were accepted by neighbouring countries. Lebanon, with a population of 6 million, accepted 1 million Syrian refugees according to the United Nations (UNHCR 2017): given that the Lebanese government stopped registering them in 2016 actual figures could be much higher. Turkey has accepted 2.5 million Syrian refugees (Refugee Council 2018). In contrast, the UK had only accepted 5,706 Syrian refugees as of 2016 (Refugee Council 2018). In general, the majority of refugees are hosted by less affluent countries in the Global South; the top countries for accepting refugees are Turkey, Pakistan, Lebanon, Iran, Ethiopia and Jordan (UNHCR 2017). By contrast, in Europe, the number of refugees accepted is comparatively much smaller, raising questions about the level of anxiety in European countries towards the presence of refugees, in relation to the discussion above about perceived threats from racialised others.

The campaign to release Shaker Aamer (the Saudi citizen living in the UK who was imprisoned in Guantanamo Bay) was also part of our sample. News coverage in the *Daily Mail* to release him framed him in relation to national interests, as an innocent 'Briton' who was wrongfully imprisoned by the US and did not have the same rights as US citizens; there was also coverage of the involvement of British celebrities in the campaign (such as former Pink Floyd member Roger Waters). Within other contexts the *Daily Mail* is notorious for framing UK residents holding citizenship of other countries as not really British. However, the overall argument of the article was about presenting the UK as taking the higher moral high ground in relation to US foreign policy.

A similar approach was also evident in the Italian news coverage of the Iraqi situation. The sample included the weeks of June 2014 in which Isis was about to occupy Mosul and then effectively took control. The sample included an interview with Ian Bremmer, an American political scientist and president of the Eurasia Group think-tank, entitled 'US disengagement left an empty space fuelled by Jihad. War will continue in Syria too':

> destroyed, inadequately reconstructed institutions – sometimes even not reconstructed at all – or the political emptiness which followed US military withdraw, left an empty space in which militias have been able to enlarge their operational capacities. (*Corriere della Sera*, 11 June 2014)

Another article, entitled 'Bush, Obama and the Iraqi chaos: whose fault? (*Corriere della Sera*, 24 June 2014) reiterated the same interpretation of the conflict in Iraq, presenting it as the personal responsibility of former presidents. US President Obama was blamed for a 'failed politics' as for 'a possible attack on Syria' and for being 'reluctant and 'unable to engage' in a military response because of 'domestic politics concerns' in terms of unpopularity of armed intervention. Iraqi Prime Minister Al Maliki was also attacked for not being really interested in 'governing the country in unitarian and competent way', by 'going beyond sectarian divisions'. This same article also included an interview with the former German Minister of Foreign Affairs, Joschka Fisher, who opposed the 2003 US-UK invasion of Iraq. He attacked Barack Obama for his decision to withdraw troops from Iraq and not intervene in Syria, while defending him from the accusations of neoconservatives such as Dick Cheney: 'the original sin of the current chaos in the Middle East lays in the invasion of Iraq. Exchanging their desires with reality, neocons forgot that Saddam Hussein's fall would create an emptiness of power which none of them knew how to fill' (*Corriere della Sera*, 24 June 2014)

While less overtly about the actions of powerful individual leaders, British coverage of Afghanistan focused on the decision of NATO to withdraw from the region, and, in the aftermath of withdrawal, on the under-equipped state of local military and police forces in the face of violence and corruption. Such accounts framed the situation in terms of the irresponsibility of NATO's decision to leave the country to its own devices, and the sense that it was incapable of governing and policing itself. This was reflected in the following news headlines in our UK sample:

> Killing, not curing: deadly boom in counterfeit medicine in Afghanistan; Corruption and lack of border controls has opened country up to flood of substandard drugs that put poor, sick Afghans at risk. (*Guardian* 7 January 2015)

> Afghan police struggle as US watchdog finds holes in payroll data; New report reveals money intended to pay salaries may instead be bankrolling 'ghost workers' – fictional employees created to enrich police chiefs. (*Guardian* 12 January 2015)

In the Italian sample, the majority of articles published by *Corriere della Sera* focused on the risk of confusing the withdrawal of NATO troops with the end of armed violence in Afghanistan – seen as an 'enduring war' because of the asymmetric nature of warfare. This was interpreted by many commentators as poorly timed and therefore as a strategic error. One example of this was an article entitled 'In Kabul the NATO mission ends. Not the war' (9 December 2014). There seemed to be much at stake in this conflict, due to its framing as a global confrontation between the West and Islamic fundamentalism: 'a war that we should not lose' (11 January 2015). Within this perspective, some of the coverage drew attention to 'our troops' remaining in Afghanistan with the aim of supporting and training local military forces: 'Those 500 Italians in Afghanistan [engaged] in the war we forgot' (1 December 2014).

At the other end of the political spectrum, *Il Giornale*[2] provided a rather different interpretation of the same events and issues. In the name of 'realism', the newspaper (perhaps unintentionally) revealed aspects of amnesia within official narratives about the war in Afghanistan. This involved blatant attempts to reclaim the Western imperial role as essentially benign. The 'silent withdrawal' from the country therefore became the occasion to blame the former centre-left government for avoiding any discussion about the war, in order to avoid accountability for poor outcomes (9 December 2014). *Il Giornale* included many news articles about the 'young Italian soldiers' who died 'in order to give hope to the Afghan people' and thus deserved 'a more decent ending of their mission'. Articles also focused on the 'great hypocrisy' of wanting to disguise war as a 'peace mission' (31 December 2014). Echoing the perspectives of far-right authors such as Oriana Fallaci, the articles also accused the West of renouncing its historical superiority as a beacon of civilisation ('being on the right side of history' (9 January 2015) in contrast to the 'barbarity' of Islam. Withdrawal from Afghanistan was therefore a mistake because a highly co-ordinated 'Global Jihad is at war against the West' (10 January 2015). Military interventions are, from this perspective, purely military and cannot create lasting stability in the region: 'Exporting democracy in the Islamic world is impossible because of an unbridgeable civilisation divide' (11 January 2015).

Eritrea and postcolonial absence

While both the *Guardian* and the *Daily Mail* in the UK only covered certain conflicts in the world – such as Iraq, Afghanistan or Syria – in which British governments and troops have been engaged, other countries such as Eritrea were barely covered. Aside from sensational comments about Eritrea being the 'North Korea of Africa' (*Guardian* 26 October 2016) there was little explanation of the oppressive regime in the country, the causes and effects of the war with Ethiopia, or the indefinite military service which had led many people to flee. The absence of Eritrea from the UK media landscape becomes even more questionable in the context of the growing Eritrean diaspora in the country, increasing from 6,561 to 17,705 UK residents between 2001 and 2011, according to census data (Office for National Statistics 2013), and the Eritreans being one of the top nationalities for asylum claim, before the door was effectively closed (Right to Remain 2017).

In Italy, according to historian Alessandro Triulzi, during the 2000s Eritrea has recaptured public attention within the so-called 'New Italian Epic', as the literary group Wu Ming defines a body of literary works written after the Italian institutional and political crises of 1993. This trend may be understood as a 'reaction to a disillusioned Italian society, fighting against the declining economic power and political identity of the nation by setting in motion dreams and fantasies bred during the colonial period' (Triulzi 2012: 108). The nostalgia surrounding Eritrea as the first Italian colony (*colonia primigenia*) did not encourage public awareness of the current conditions of the country under President Isaias Afewerki, nor with the undermining of the Independence process under his authoritarian rule (Drudi and Omizzolo 2015). Eritrea entered the mainstream media only in response to deadly shipwrecks in the Mediterranean with many Eritrean victims, although through the nostalgic lens described above.

The only article in our UK sample was a call for user-generated contents on the *GuardianWitness* section, entitled 'Outside looking in: what's it like to be Eritrean living abroad?', soliciting perspectives from the Eritrean diaspora in the UK and elsewhere:

> What does it mean to be Eritrean? How do you stay in touch with your culture and customs when living in a foreign country? Are you an active member of the Eritrean community? Tell us more about your role, whether it's supporting cyclists, running radio programmes or mobilising online. We'd also like to know the hardest thing about living away from your homeland and what people, or the media, frequently misunderstand about it. (*GuardianWitness* August 2015)

Many comments focused on the legacies of the conflict between Eritrea and Ethiopia, with different perspectives:

> The cultural, linguistic, ethnic and historical closeness of the Eritrean and Ethiopian peoples could have become an asset for both Eritreans and Ethiopians. But the hard-heartedness of the two regimes in power is making it a liability for both peoples, and especially for Eritrean refugees.
>
> Eritreans, as with most other people in the world, are blinded with identity politics and its prime manifestation patriotism. (*Guardian-Witness* August 2015)

These insights were conspicuous in relation to the absence of these perspectives elsewhere, or else their circumscription (where Eritreans were only quoted as witnesses to atrocities), and the role that this plays in constructing white amnesia and postcolonial innocence. Three articles were published by *Corriere della Sera* framing Eritrea as the former Italian colony that became Africa's prison and the former colony which remained in Italians' hearts, in response to deadly shipwrecks with many Eritrean victims. These articles appeared on 7 April 2011 ('Desperate people fleeing from dictatorship in the former first Italian colony'), 4 October 2011 ('Torture, arrests, forced labour: the flight from the Eritrean Inferno') and 27 April 2015 ('Eritrea, 2,000 flee each month'). On the conservative end of the Italian media landscape, since 2013 *Il Giornale* has published less than 20 articles mentioning Eritrea, none of which discussed the internal political situation in detail. Instead, these articles primarily focused on immigration issues, such as the involvement of Eritreans in shipwrecks, search and rescue operations, or other events related to migration, as well as the persecution of Christians.

Postcolonial innocence and the benevolent role of European nations

If European nations are seen to bear no responsibility for global conflicts and inequalities, this self-perception as 'innocent' therefore enables them to present themselves as essentially generous and benevolent towards refugees, as they owe them nothing. This in turn makes it easier for anti-immigrant commentators to present refugees as abusers of this benevolence. This perspective is expressed by former Italian Prime Minister Matteo Renzi in his latest book (*Forward! Why Italy is not staying behind*), echoing the traditional formulas of right-wing anti-immigrant movements:

> We would like to free ourselves from a certain kind of *sense of guilt*. We do not have the *moral duty* to welcome in Italy all the people who are worst off. If this would happen, it would be an ethical, political, social and finally also an economic *disaster*. We do not have the duty to welcome them, let's repeat it again. And yes, we have

> the moral duty to save them, if they risk their lives at sea. And, beyond this, we have the moral duty to help them – but to really help them – *at home*. (Renzi 2017, emphasis added)

Significantly, an opinion poll at the time of this statement revealed that 48% of respondents considered the statement 'let's help them at home' to be a simple expression of common sense, with 52% among supporters of Renzi's party, the Democratic Party, agreeing. 24% of respondents considered this expression to be apolitical, while only 17% considered it to be a specifically right-wing statement (*Huffington Post* 2017).

This self-perception of European nations as essentially benevolent is the counterpart of the obsession with the threats posed by racialised outsiders. Both are present in the coexistence of securitarian and humanitarian concerns within media representations of search and rescue operations in the Mediterranean (Cuttitta 2018). European states do not perceive themselves as having any legal obligations towards people on the move who risk their lives at sea. Instead, search and rescue operations are presented as top-down gestures of generosity and goodwill. This self-perception also deprives migrants of any autonomous agency or voice, as 'we' saved them, and therefore they should be eternally grateful to their 'saviours'.

As the 'migration crisis' continued to persist, the self-perception of being under siege intensified, justifying the criminalisation of NGOs engaged in search and rescue operations. Within this context, search and rescue operations in the Mediterranean have been vilified as a 'pull factor' for migrations, paradoxically blamed for loss of life, despite lack of evidence (Forensic Oceanography & Watch the Med 2016). This meant that humanitarian efforts eventually came under suspicion. As recently stated by the former Italian Minister of the Interior on his Facebook profile:

> As a father of two children, I do not want that other children will be put on a dinghy and die in the Mediterranean because someone deludes them saying that in Italy there are jobs and homes for

everyone. I'm sick and tired of this. (Matteo Salvini, speech in Senate, 13 June 2018)

'Those defending these positions usually present themselves as the "true humanitarians", while blaming NGOs and the "professionals of humanitarianism" engaged in saving lives at sea as acting as a "pull factor", thus increasing departures and the final death toll' (Guerzoni 2018). Moreover, the humanitarian motives of NGOs in the Mediterranean came under question, based on unconfirmed rumours of collusion with human traffickers and with the 'business of co-operatives' operating in the reception system.[3] More generally, the role of co-operatives was discredited following the scandal of *Mafia capitale* which revealed cases of corruption and the involvement of organised crime in the asylum system.[4]

As clearly stated by the former Italian Minister of the Interior, 'our aim is to protect the external border, not to share the problem among European countries but to solve the problem at the source' (Kirchgaessner 2018). In practice, this means enforcing agreements with transit countries such as Libya in order to block migrant boats from entering international waters, holding people in detention centres, then eventually deporting them. In reality, Italian governments of all political orientation tried to solve the problem 'at the source' by signing 'agreements of co-operation' with Libya (Paoletti 2010; Cuttitta 2014), drawing on Italy/Libya colonial and postcolonial ties (Brambilla 2014).

The Italian-Libyan agreement offers a model for similar deals with other African countries of origin and transit, linking economic aid and military support to border controls in order to prevent irregular migration and human trafficking.[5] The Italian military mission in Niger approved by the Parliament in January 2018 is typical of these initiatives. The mission will see around 470 Italian troops join the French and US soldiers already stationed there to help President Mahamadou Issoufou better fight insurgents and control the country's borders. On 24 December 2017, during a

Christmas Eve meeting with the Italian soldiers engaged in the European border control mission 'Sophia', former Italian Prime Minister Paolo Gentiloni promised the mission would 'guarantee stability in the country and fight illegal trafficking of migrants and terrorism' (*Il Messaggero* 24 December 2017). To avoid accusations of militarism or even neo-colonialism, former Defence Minister Roberta Pinotti clarified that 'this is a training mission in response to a request from Niger, not a combat mission'. The Five Star Movement, then still in the opposition, attacked the centre-left government for 'supporting risky neo-colonial interests' (*Il Fatto Quotidiano* 17 January 2018).

Postcolonial innocence and siege mentalities

The assumption that Western nations hold no responsibility for global conflicts which lead people to flee their countries underpinned fears that refugees would 'bring the war home' and import social conflict into harmonious and homogeneous Western societies. According to this logic, the most appropriate response is military self-defence and the criminalisation of 'solidarity with the enemy'. Militaristic language became increasingly common in characterising the 'European migration crisis' as a chaotic flood and even as an invasion, while moral panics proliferated about the escalating numbers of migrants, sometimes even including figures of those who had not yet left but were considering doing so. In early October 2015, as emotionally charged images of Alan Kurdi were still vivid in the mind of many Europeans, the President of the European Council, Donald Tusk, described the migrants as a 'great tide' that has 'flooded into Europe' producing 'chaos' that needs to be 'stemmed and managed'. He also abruptly claimed, probably alluding to the Turkish government or to Isis: 'We are slowly becoming witnesses to the birth of a new form of political pressure. Some even call it a kind of a new hybrid war, in which migratory waves have become a tool, a weapon against neighbours' (Holehouse

2015). Within such an approach, deaths at the border may be normalised and accepted as collateral damage, or even used as a measure of 'deterrence' against further attempts to enter the EU. This approach was implicit in the official discourses put forward in 2014 by the leaders of the UK government and Frontex blaming the search and rescue operation *Mare Nostrum* for encouraging refugees to come to Europe. Moreover, statistical analyses of absolute and relative mortality risks in the Mediterranean have now challenged these deterrence-oriented policy narratives (Steinhilper and Gruijters 2018).

In Italy, these invasion narratives, which had been previously limited to right-wing movements and media channels, began to receive increasing attention from the mainstream media, eventually becoming hegemonic common sense. These narratives were supported by conspiracy theories about white genocide and global elites trying to import cheap labour who would undercut wages. Similar to Hungary (Juhász et al. 2017), conspiracies often centred on billionaire and philanthropist George Soros, because of the role of his Open Society Foundation in funding many NGOs engaged in protecting migrants' rights.

If Europe is under siege, Italy is seen to be particularly at risk because of its exposed geographical position on the Mediterranean. This perception of Italy's vulnerability is also the unintended result of the media attention given to search and rescue operations. During the first ten months of 2015, there was an unprecedented level of news coverage in Italian print and broadcast media relating to the refugee crisis, with headlines devoted to it by major newspapers increasing by 70–180%, a peak of 80% more reporting in print media and a 250% higher frequency in broadcasting compared to the previous year (Carta di Roma 2015). In the absence of analysis, this stream of images of people at sea contributes to the narrative that everyone is coming to Italy (a smaller-scale version of the narrative about everyone coming to Europe).

Institutional failures and distrust

The contradictions between the siege mentality and the self-perceptions of Western nations as essentially innocent and benevolent fed increasingly prevalent narratives of global and national institutions as unstable and ineffective, both in dealing with international conflicts, and with the migration flows resulting from them. This produced widespread perceptions of the governance of migration as dysfunctional, exemplifying the contradictions and inadequacies of nation-states within a globalising world (Brown 2010). Attempts by states to both meet the demands of neoliberal globalisation and address local concerns about immigration has produced increasingly harsh rhetoric and policies, which makes life difficult for many immigrants – but also has not reduced migration flows. For example, since 2010, the UK government have kept a target to cut net immigration (meaning the balance between immigration and emigration) to the tens of thousands. They have failed to meet this target every year and could not in fact practically meet it without causing serious damage to the economy (Centre for Economics and Business Research 2017). However, despite being unable to meet this target they were also unwilling to renounce it. In relation to asylum policies and rhetoric, governments were enmeshed in contradictions between humanitarian obligations and securitarian approaches. In part as a result of these contradictions, they were incapable of preventing deaths at sea, efficiently processing asylum applications or supporting refugees and enabling them to integrate. These failures and contradictions created a sense of radical distrust, which in turn fuelled populist anti-immigrant politics.

For migrants and their supporters, the most generous interpretation of this situation is about the inadequate resources of governments (already stretched by austerity measures). At the worst it represents organised state cruelty: a deliberate attempt to under-fund support systems in order to be seen as tough on immigration and develop immigration systems which were designed for people, particularly those from poorer countries of the Global South, to fail. For those opposed to immigration, governments are failing to meaningfully stem the flow of people or reverse the visible signs of cultural change, despite the harsh messaging and tough policies. This means that the failures of migration systems have become broader symbols for the breakdown of governance. We will now discuss how this played out in UK and Italian media.

In the UK, coverage of Eritrea in the *Daily Mail* frequently focused on outrage at foreign aid spending in the region, which was presented from *taking* money from British taxpayers and giving it to corrupt regimes outside the West, with the UK, and by extension British taxpayers, presented as innocent and gullible victims of this swindle. This was exemplified by articles entitled 'Britain's aid bill may soar' (3 April 2015) and 'Britain spends more on foreign aid than any other EU nation' (5 January 2016). Both articles presented the UK as a naïve and defenceless victim being fleeced by other countries, and which was forced to do so by the EU. It was suggested that the money was not going to those who needed it and was instead supporting corrupt regimes. Politicians were also quoted as saying that during a period of austerity, money should be supporting people in the UK (such as flood victims) rather than those in other countries. Such articles tried to create a simple equivalence between national citizen-taxpayers and recipients of state money. According to this logic, the only legitimate or decent way to spend money was locally, with any aid money sent to the EU or other countries framed as theft and deception. Unsurprisingly, Brexit was suggested as the solution so that British money would only be paid to British people. This became more explicit in below-the-line comments, which repeatedly called for voting to leave the EU and support for the UK Independence Party – which promised to restore the equivalence of national citizen-taxpayer and recipient of state funding.

These narratives which present the UK as the victim and as isolated from global contexts are blind to the larger historical context which would lead countries such as Eritrea to be recipients of foreign aid in the first place. This includes legacies of colonial plunder (Eritrea was colonised by both the UK and Italy) as well as more recent global inequalities. There is therefore a particular irony in presenting the UK as a victim of exploitation by other countries, as well as a disavowal of responsibility around the UK's present and historical role in global geopolitics.

Refugees as cover for terrorism

Since the Paris attacks on 13 November 2015 the European migration crisis has also been imbricated in narratives about the threat of terrorism. Migration is understood to be 'a form of barbarian warfare that threatens the European Union' and 'every migrant is a potential terrorist and vice versa' (Nail 2016: 158). However, in the Italian media, moral panics around foreign fighters and 'home-grown extremists' travelling under cover amongst refugees predated the Paris attack. For example, reporting on an alleged statement by the Italian ambassador at Tripoli, one of the first headlines on this issue appeared on 27 July 2014 in *Il Tempo*, a right-wing media outlet: 'Risk of Jihadists on illegal aliens' boats'. The same newspaper repeatedly drew attention to this 'scoop', making reference to different sources: 'This is how veterans of Syria war come back to fight in Europe' (27 July 2014); 'Eurojust reveals: Isis militants under cover of boat people' (7 July 2015).

In the summer of 2016, after the apparent defeat of Isis in Libya, new rumours of terrorists infiltrating refugee groups were published in mainstream news outlets such as *La Repubblica*. For example, a news article entitled 'Intelligence alarm: terrorists are arriving among boat people' reported statements released by the President of the Italian Parliamentary Committee for the Intelligence and Security Services and for State Secret Control:

> For a long time, it has been highly unlikely, if not impossible, for Daesh to permit its affiliates to travel on migrant boats, exposing

> them to the objectively high risks of the sea-crossing after having invested time and money in them. Today we are in the middle of chaos. On the flight from Libya, those who are not going South could even try to reach Europe across the sea. They are mavericks, people in disarray. The point is to understand their intentions: just disappearing or keeping the fight in the name of their cause? (*Repubblica.it* 13 August 2016).

These stories entered mainstream news after reports of a Tunisian citizen who arrived in Italy by boat in 2011 as a minor, then was denied asylum, imprisoned and ordered to leave the country. He then killed twelve people in the attack on the Christmas market in Berlin in December 2016. In January 2017 the Italian Department of Public Security, which has authority over the police, reassured the public that there was no confirmation of fifty Isis fighters who were prepared to carry out terrorist attacks landing on the Italian coast. During the police investigations, a small number of Tunisian citizens without papers were deported. Moreover, after our sampling period Tunisian people smuggling was still a current news item. A prosecutor in charge of investigating Tunisian 'ghost landings'[6] in Agrigento, Sicily, pointed out that boats from Tunisia are very different to the vessels used by Libyan people smugglers: 'The boats they travel with have nothing to do with the crumbling migrant boats coming from Libya. The Tunisians arrive with excellent boats, sturdy and sailed by experts who know the sea well' (Tondo and Messina 2018).

A similar conspiracy news story was reported by *La Stampa* about Isis militants manipulating the flows of refugees coming from Libya to destabilise Europe (4 August 2016). A 'scoop' was first published by *Il Giornale* in an article entitled 'Isis's menace: if you strike us, we will send over 500,000 migrants' (17 February 2015). The story was allegedly based on phone conversations which were recorded by Italian intelligence services. However, the existence of the phone conversations was never confirmed, nor was there any attempt to check the figure of 500,000 against the actual number of people coming to Europe via the Mediterranean.

The failures of the EU and the abandonment of Italy

These conspiracies and moral panics contribute to perceptions of migration governance as a failure and of governments being duped by terrorists, fraudsters and (in the case of Italy) organised crime networks. European institutions are portrayed as indifferent at best or, at worst, as allies and silent supporters of global elites. They are therefore blamed for having left Italy alone to deal with the emergency – a narrative that populist politicians have capitalised on, as discussed below. However, despite the conspiratorial nature of such narratives, it is important to acknowledge that this resentment draws on the undeniable failures of distributing refugees amongst EU member states, which has left Southern European countries such as Italy facing the greatest burden. Another contributing factor is the opposition of core EU states to renegotiating the Dublin Regulation[7] – which then places greater pressure on Italy due to its geographical location as a port of first entry.

These narratives about Italy's abandonment are common across the political spectrum. For example, popular centre-left politicians such as Giuliano Pisapia (the former mayor of Milan), was among the first to mobilise this conventionally right-wing, Eurosceptic argument:

> Milan did its part and will continue to do so. But we cannot afford more than this. Considering that Europe left us alone, it will be necessary to redistribute people among Italian regions, in proportion to the number of residents and in relation to the effective capacity to provide a first and dignified hospitality. (Leggo.it, 15 June 2015)

More recently, this narrative has been used by the current Italian government to justify the decision to ban the Aquarius migrant rescue ship with 629 people on board from docking at Italian ports. Prime Minister Giuseppe Conte stated that 'Europe is not showing solidarity', adding that 'Italy has to deal with the problem' of human trafficking and migration flows 'all by itself.' Conte also pointed out that some EU states, such as Malta, shut their borders and refused to co-operate with Italy.

Within such narratives, European institutions are ineffectual: deaths at sea continue to occur and foreign aid money lines the pockets of corrupt dictators. The lofty claims about international co-operation only mask the selfishness of wealthy Northern and Western European nations who do not want to deal with the influx of refugees. In the most conspiratorial of such narratives, European institutions only represent the interests of global elites who do not have the interests of citizens at heart. The logical conclusion is that the only way to restore trust is to 'take back control', as in the slogan of the Vote Leave campaign in the UK. However, such narratives ignore the larger historical context which would lead some countries to need foreign aid or the conditions which would lead their citizens to flee. They also disavow the responsibility that Italy, the UK or other European countries have played within global geopolitics which would lead countries such as Eritrea to be in this dire situation. To acknowledge this responsibility troubles the seductive logic of white amnesia and claims to victimhood.

Countering postcolonial innocence and white amnesia

The rest of the chapter explores resources for countering postcolonial innocence, and specifically what can be learnt from the experiences of migrants. We carried out interviews and workshop activities with migrants in Nottingham and Birmingham, Bologna and Pisa, in which they discussed their experiences in the UK and in Italy, and they analysed the situations in the countries they had left and the media coverage of conflicts and migration. In doing so, we were trying to do two things: to get the direct perspectives of asylum seekers and refugees on the UK and Italy, and on the media representation of their countries and of themselves, as they are rarely asked for their opinion. We were also trying to engage with them in other ways rather than asking them for testimonials of their migration journeys, which they are frequently asked to do by both the media and public authorities in order to prove their deservingness of protection (discussed further in chapter 5).

We asked participants in our project to reflect on how they were being constructed as migrants by the state and members of society, and ways in which this could be challenged. Our participants were refugees from a variety of countries; some had fled war and repressive regimes; others were escaping poverty or had fallen through the cracks of the immigration system. They had lived in the UK and Italy for varying periods of time. The process began with interviews in which we invited participants to reflect on moments when they felt they were being treated as migrants; we also asked them about the resources they used to survive the hardships of the asylum system, as well as their views on how the conflicts in their countries could be resolved. As many of the countries they had left (Sudan, Eritrea, Zimbabwe, etc.) had long histories of colonialism and foreign intervention, one of the common themes within these conversations was the still-present cultural memory of these legacies. This provided a framework for the respondents to understand continued global inequality, and for them to map their personal experiences and analyses of the political situations of the countries they had left into this.

Legacies of Empire

When asked about the situation in the countries they had left and how it could be resolved, our respondents saw the situation in their countries as a direct outcome of colonial legacies:

> They were identifying the potential of that country [in Zimbabwe] to contribute to the economy of the United Kingdom. That is when the problems started.
>
> [After independence] people started fighting among themselves again over the resources that were in the country. But then which weapons were they using to fight among themselves? Zimbabwe doesn't make a single gun. We fought among ourselves using guns made in the UK, made in the Soviet Union, made in Europe (London, April 2017).

Conflict, poverty and corruption were perceived by our respondents as directly implicated in global inequality, particularly the legacies of colonial exploitation and the arms trade.

In a group discussion, one of our respondents shared an internet meme including a quote from Lord Thomas Babington MacAulay, which was supposedly delivered to the British Parliament in 1835 and justified the introduction of Western culture into India in connection with British colonisation (MacAulay was in fact a proponent of the belief that indigenous cultures should be eliminated through the colonial education system):

> I have travelled across the length and breadth of India and I have not seen one person who is a beggar, who is a thief. Such wealth I have seen in this country. Such high moral values, people of such calibre that I do not think that we would ever conquer this country unless we break the backbone of this nation which is her spiritual and cultural heritage, and therefore I propose that we replace her old, ancient education system, her culture, if the Africans think that all that is foreign and English is good and greater than their own they will lose their self-esteem, their native culture, and will become what we want then, a truly dominated nation.

While the speech was originally about India, the internet meme replaced 'India' with 'Africa'. It is debatable whether MacAulay had in fact given that speech, when historical accounts demonstrate he was not in the UK on that day (Mitra 2017); however, the content of the speech is consistent with MacAulay's racist and imperialist worldview (Mitra 2017). The sharing of the quote reflects the role played by social media as a news source, but also struck a chord with personal experiences. For example, the quote provoked one respondent to relate corruption in the country she had left to legacies of colonialism:

> And it's so steeped in our system. Because I was growing up, although the system had changed, it's still there within the people where the moral code is, you look after each other. The community look after

> each other. But it's just the level of the government, the people who are voted in, who are just out there to get what they want, not to look after their own people. (Focus group discussion, Nottingham, 19 April 2017)

Like the other participants, she saw the government in the country she had left as being self-serving, as 'just out there to get what they want', which she contrasted with the community looking after each other – which she saw as having survived colonial rule (against all odds).

How legacies of colonialism determine who has access to mobility

Our participants understood the differential expectations which determine who has mobility and who does not, and who is expected to integrate or who does not in relation to legacies of colonialism. This was generally reflective of a system in which transnational elites can move easily, in contrast to the difficulties experienced by ordinary people moving across borders. As Ghasan Hage observes:

> In apartheid fashion, these two experiences delineate two separate realities or worlds that coexist within the same global space. On the one hand, we have a world where a 'third-world-looking' transnational working class and underclass live and are made to feel that national borders are exceptionally important and difficult to cross. In this world, visas, checkpoints, searches, investigations, interviews, immigration bureaucracies, refusal of permission to cross, language problems, embassy queues, cost of travel, and the like all combine to make national borders appear salient and important realities. On the other hand, we have a world experienced as open, in which people move smoothly across national borders, experiencing the world as almost borderless. This is the experience enjoyed by the largely White upper classes, who are made to feel truly at home in the world. (Hage 2017)

Our respondents were at the sharpest end of the immigration system and had the least mobility of all; they experienced the most rigid bureaucratic structures and the greatest restrictions on their day-to-day experience; in the UK, they did not even have the right to work. This double standard was not lost on them:

> So how could you stand up and say that Mugabe is evil when you're still supporting ... You're letting him come to your conference. You're letting him come to anything. But you're barring a poor old grandmother who is running away from being tortured, her family being executed, and all that. But you're letting in the people who are responsible for that atrocity. So what does it say about your moral values and what you are selling to the ... you know. (Focus group discussion, Nottingham, 19 April 2017)

There have been recent controversies about the use of 'golden visa' schemes in which ultra-wealthy individuals can have fast-tracked permanent residency in exchange for investing large sums in the country. Such schemes exist in the UK, Italy and other Western nations, despite concerns that they facilitate corruption and organised crime. However, the golden visas are only the most obvious example of the inequalities within the immigration system. The contrast between the ease with which the ultra-wealthy can access permanent residency within Western nations and the difficulties faced by those in the asylum system is one of the hypocrisies flagged up by the participant, particularly when accompanied by official denunciations of corruption in Africa.

Throughout our project, including in the responses to our survey of media use (discussed in chapter 2), we were reminded of the erasure of imperial histories and debts underlying European affluence. One outcome of this erasure was a contradictory approach to population movement building on histories of colonialism and Empire and the celebration of some travel as adventure, philanthropy or exploration. In particular, participants pointed to the continuing movement of Europeans and those of European descent across the world and the reception granted to Europeans in movement. They contrasted this with their own lack of mobility and continual scrutiny: both the restrictions they faced in their dealings with the immigration system, but also the harsh treatment and inflammatory rhetoric directed towards immigrants from outside Europe. This issue arose repeatedly in our workshops and discussions, often closely linked to comments on imperial histories and the wilful amnesia of European subjects in relation to histories of colonial expropriation.

As with some of the other discussions, these contradictions around population movement also were imbricated within processes of racialisation. It seemed that light-skinned Europeans continued to feel an entitlement to move around the world at will and to be welcomed when they arrived. Ironically, some of our discussions indicated that the 'rest of the world' colluded with this view, also, it is implied, privileging whiteness:

> I: Does it work the other way? What if Europeans got to Africa?
>
> R2: We don't call them migrants.
>
> R1: We welcome them.
>
> R2: We don't even call them migrants, we take them as family. Just because you are strange, they are new people, we are just happy to see them.
>
> R1: They are white, so we welcome them.
>
> R2: We want them to even stay, that is the difference. (Nottingham, 19 April 2017)

White Europeans were welcomed and even treated as family – and then, historically went on to plunder and exploit. Due to continuing global inequalities (many of which are legacies of colonial exploitation), they still continue to be welcomed as business people, state officials, philanthropists, and so on.

A related contradiction was the categorisation of people as expats rather than as immigrants. When asked about how to define an expat in contrast to a migrant, an expat was imagined by one of the participants as someone who was continually on the move, and whose movement across borders was easier and more carefree:

> I: There is a difference between a migrant and like an expatriate, because it sounds like that is what you are talking about.
>
> R: Yes, because an expatriate, you are just, oh I am going. (Nottingham, 19 April 2017)

Our participants pointed to the discrepancy between the mobility enjoyed by expats in contrast with their absolute lack of mobility (they could not leave the country while waiting for their claims to be processed). There was a sense that expats did not have to demonstrate that they were learning English or integrating into society – in contrast to migrants who must continually demonstrate this, with a sense that it is never enough. The distinction between expat and migrant was racialised in that whiteness was associated with the freedoms and status of being an expat, in terms of being able to move freely and being welcome everywhere (a kind of universal mobile subject):

> I could also see that that label [expat] if a white person comes to Nigeria, that person is an expatriate if it is not [a] white person then you are a migrant. You don't get them getting a label of migrants in Nigeria. (Nottingham, 19 April 2017)

Although the participant refers to labelling, it is not only a question of language, but also of the racialisation processes and geopolitical power relations which would lead white people in Nigeria to be perceived as expats (and afforded those privileges) while a Nigerian in a Western country would be treated as a migrant.

How does this relate to white amnesia or postcolonial innocence? There is a sense that for some (particularly transnational elites), the freedom to move across borders is taken as normal. This includes the privileges afforded to politicians (including despots such as Mugabe), courted by Western governments in search of international trade or diplomatic links, or the generous terms offered by golden visas and other similar schemes As the last quote suggests, there may also be some internalisation of racial hierarchies within their countries. This is different from the restrictions faced by those on work, study or family visas, or – as has been discussed – the difficulties faced by our participants.

Such hierarchies reflect the imbrication of immigration regimes within neoliberal economics as a 'multiplication of labour' (Mezzadra and Nielson 2013). However, the continuities between neoliberal economics and colonial legacies – particularly how these inequalities play out within immigration regimes – are rarely discussed. It is taken for granted that citizens within Western countries and the elites of non-Western countries can move easily but that restrictions – and in the case of citizens of certain countries, quite heavy ones – are put in place for others. The acceptance of this situation can be understood as a form of post-imperial amnesia, because it involves ignoring the legacies of oppression that have produced it. What is significant is that by asking why Mugabe could travel freely but an elderly lady fleeing his regime cannot, *in response to a discussion about the legacies of British colonialism* suggests that participants are drawing links between the two.

Conclusion

The postcolonial representation of population movement and settlement as a 'migration crisis' plays a significant role in official and popular attitudes towards immigration and migrants, particularly arguments in favour of stricter border controls. In a recent poll, almost 60% of Italian respondents said it was right to shut their ports to ships transporting migrants from Africa, and 68% said former Minister Matteo Salvini was correct to stand up to the EU on the issue (Anastasi et al. 2018).

Far from preventing deaths, borders play an active role in people losing their lives. Our analyses of media representations of war attempt to explore the structural, neo-colonial violence (such as the wars in Iraq and Afghanistan, or the ongoing political repression in Eritrea) which produces displacement in which people risk their lives. The first phase of displacement consists of the expulsion of impoverished communities, or those who have been subject to military invasions; the second phase involves the securitisation and militarisation of borders, including practices of *refoulement*, expulsion and detention. What such perspectives misunderstand is the agency of migrants and the meaning of their claim for free movement across borders. As Ghassan Hage observes, 'They are like escaping slaves attempting to free themselves from the increasingly suffocating global order of apartheid by traveling in its shadows and through its cracks. (Hage 2017). Hage adds that, tellingly 'when caught, they are increasingly caged and treated like escaped slaves' (Hage 2017).

To understand racism and xenophobia today, we need to consider the inability to come to terms with these legacies, and the still-persistent sense of superiority within Britain, Italy and other Western nations in relation to other parts of the world. This sense of superiority makes it difficult to imagine 'others' in contexts of war, and to perceive international conflicts as resulting from the actions of great men, with the views of those outside the West being of little consequence Our respondents were well aware of this situation. They discussed how little was understood of the situation outside the West; they also saw continuities between colonial histories, neoliberal bordering regimes and the inequalities of the immigration system that made it easy for some to move across borders and made it more comparatively more restrictive for others.

So how can this be countered? As Ida Danewid asks, how might we rethink global ethics and solidarity on the basis of 'shared, intertwined histories that arise out of the colonial past and the neo-colonial present' (2017: 1681)? In the interviews and workshops, there were glimpses of alternative values and systems, which could also be considered resources for challenging white amnesia and postcolonial innocence. For example, one of the interviewees offered suggestions about what this might look like:

> UK people, I mean British, I mean English people, themselves, they move around the world freely. They should accept other people coming to them freely and once there's rules and laws they should be welcoming others because people, they are welcoming English people elsewhere. (Birmingham, 16 February 2017)

He suggests an alternative system in which people could move freely between countries 'once there's rules and laws'. Notably, he implies that these rules and laws would be applied to everyone equally, regardless of country of origin. This is in marked contrast to the current system of differential rights to mobility that forms the basis of the immigration system, which, as we have argued, is a product of colonial legacies and racial hierarchies.

Notes

1 Developed and adopted by the European Commission in May 2015 as part of the immediate action to assist Member States located at the external EU border, the so-called Hotspot approach consists of the co-operation on the ground between European Asylum Support Office (EASO), the European Border and Coast Guard Agency (Frontex), Europol and Eurojust with the authorities of Italy and Greece, with the aim to fulfil their obligations under EU law. The operational support provided under the Hotspot approach focuses on registration, identification, fingerprinting (even with the use of force, if necessary) and support of asylum seekers, as well as relocation and return operations. Those claiming asylum will be channelled into an asylum procedure, while those who are considered 'not in need of protection' will be returned as irregular migrants: this mechanism of triage, like the forced taking of fingerprints, has been strongly criticised by human rights organisations (Amnesty International 2016; Capitani 2016; ECRE et al. 2016).

2 *Il Giornale* is owned by the Berlusconi family and has a right-wing, strongly conservative and neo-liberal political orientation.

3 In Italy, the expression 'business of co-operatives' has become common as a derogatory definition of the entire economy related to the asylum reception system, often managed by co-operative enterprises which are under contract by governmental district authorities (*Prefetture*).
4 For details of this coverage see *Il Fatto Quotidiano*'s coverage of the topic at: https://www.ilfattoquotidiano.it/tag/mafia-capitale/.
5 The text of the agreement is available in English at http://eumigration lawblog.eu/wp-content/uploads/2017/10/MEMORANDUM_translation_finalversion.doc.pdf.
6 'Ghost landings' is a term used by the local Italian authorities to refer to the arrival of Tunisians on the coast during night-time on small boats; the passengers then disappear into the countryside to avoid capture by the coast guard and the police.
7 The Dublin Regulation (also known as Regulation 604/2013 or as the Dublin III Regulation) is an EU regulation which is based on the principle that that the first country of entry be responsible for the asylum process, and therefore for the reception of all asylum seekers. As a response to the 'refugee crisis', in May 2016 the European Commission presented a draft proposal to reform the Dublin System, including 'reallocation mechanisms' to deal with situations when countries are handling a 'disproportionate number' of asylum applications.

Interlude 1

Global power and media absences

During interviews with migrants in the UK and Italy, we asked how they felt about the media coverage of the countries they had left, both by international news media and by the local media in their countries. Participants were generally quite critical of news media, as in the following reflection on the state of news:

> So it's like the world of journalism has gone upside down. They spend more time researching about celebrity news and making it more legitimate than the actual news that need to be told. (Nottingham, 19 April 2017)

Participants were also aware of the limitations of the official news coverage in of their countries of origin. They drew attention to the global political economy of media and the misrepresentation or under-representation of countries outside the West. They also expressed concerns about the misrepresentation and lack of representation of ethnic minorities:

> I think in this day, in this digital age, when technology is in every corner of the world, news organisations must avoid parachuting people to Africa to report African stories from their own perspective. Why don't you give those Africans a chance to tell their own stories and link up with the media organisations in the UK? (London, 15 March 2017)

> Look at the news tonight, look, identify the number of stories that will be about Black people, only maybe if a Black person has committed a crime are they going to feature, other than that you won't hear anything about us. Are we not there? Are we not five per cent of the community? Why is five per cent of the news not dedicated to us? (London, 15 March 2017)

In Italy, some of the people we interviewed had been established in the country for two to five years. They provided further critical insights on Italian newspapers and on how they cover news from their country of origin, but also on the media in their country of origin.

For example, one Eritrean migrant was very aware of the role media played in the long war between Ethiopia and Eritrea after Eritrea achieved independence, as well as attempts by the Eritrean regime to censor the press. This experience made him critical of media and distrustful of state power:

> Well, we went to war because they overwhelmed us with TV, newspapers and radio telling everyone 'Ethiopia is about to invade us. They invade us!' So our mothers sent their sons as soldiers to war. The war ends, and what? Many said 'Let's come back to politics and build our democracy. He did not answer to these claims, the President. Fifteen ministers and thirty journalists wrote a letter to ask for the democratisation of social and political life in Eritrea. He received the letter but on the 18 September 2001 those who wrote it disappeared. *He* made them disappear. (Bologna, 22 March 2017)

Asked about Italian news media coverage on Eritrea, he was very clear:

> Newspapers or TV newscasts do not talk about it. At least I didn't notice it during the two years I'm in Italy now. Who talks about Eritrea? Except for some interested journalist, or some specialised magazines, no one. There are no public debates. No Eritrean voices to be heard. If you go on the street and ask people, one in ten knows that Eritreans are leaving the country and arriving in Italy, but they do not know why. (Bologna, 22 March 2017)

Another interviewee from Afghanistan provided a clear-cut assessment on the Eurocentric logic inspiring the changing priorities of news media in Italy, in relation to regions and conflicts outside of Europe:

> I read news about Afghanistan every day. It's my birth country. Previously the media talked a lot about Afghanistan, maybe because after 2001 it was one of the few countries where there was a war and Italian soldiers were involved. Year after year, the focus of the mainstream media changed – moving from Iraq to Syria, and more recently to Libya – as now your interests are there. And yet, if you read more credible magazines, like *Internazionale*, or some Afghan websites, you become aware that 2016 has been the most bloody year in the last decade. The war in Afghanistan was never over. People just don't talk about it any more. (Bologna, 8 February 2017)

Those we interviewed also brought a critical perspective to reading the news from the countries they had left – as in some cases it was the only way they could follow the news at all. Some were aware that within the context of authoritarian regimes the only news that was available was no better than state propaganda. They took the approach of reading it critically, 'between the lines', as this participant says, to see how it reveals insights about government strategy.

> My favourite reading news from the state-owned newspaper, the state-owned daily [in Zimbabwe], which is called *The Herald*, it's like *Pravda*, so like all romanticised propaganda basically – lies and falsehood – but they are good because they allow you to see what government strategy and policy and thoughts are if you can read between the lines. (London, 1 April 2017)

Importantly for our project, those we interviewed were aware of the limitations of news coverage of conflicts, particularly the ephemeral nature of international news and its Eurocentric perspectives which led it to under-/mis-represent both countries outside of Europe and racialised communities within own borders. The responses often involved frustration at the structures of media power and its exclusion of voices outside the West. In the pages that follow, the political critiques underpinning these frustrations is explored more fully.

2

War narratives: making sense of conflict

On 11 July 2018, an argument between then Italian Minister of Interiors, Matteo Salvini, and the former President of Italian NGO Emergency, Cecilia Strada, circulated through social media. Salvini suggested that the vast majority of migrants recently rescued in the Mediterranean were in fact people not entitled to protection, because they were not from countries at war.

> These are the nationalities of the immigrants who boarded the Italian Coast Guard vessel 'Diciotti', recovered by a previous vessel in Libyan waters: twenty-three [from] Pakistan, four Morocco, four Algeria, one Bangladesh, one Chad, two Egypt, one Ghana, ten Libya, one Nepal, seven Palestine, twelve Sudan, one Yemen. The two rioters [who started the protest] are from Ghana and Sudan. P.S. In which of those countries is there war??? (Salvini, post on Facebook, 11 June 2018)

There were also rumours that some of the migrants protested and even tried to hold a mutiny as they suspected that the vessel was bringing them back to Libya (Romano 2018; *Il Post* 2018). Cecilia Strada and many other commentators argued that Salvini's assertion had no basis in reality: in all these countries there are situations of persecution and serious harm, related to violent conflicts, all justifying the recognition of some form of international protection.

It is important to remember that one has the right to seek protection within many other circumstances than the narrowly defined 'states of war' of Salvini's assertions. In reality, for decades, the key legal concept for defining refugees has not been displacement caused by war or indiscriminate violence, but 'persecution' on specific grounds. Article 1A, Section Two of the 1951 UN Convention lays out the following criteria to be met by an asylum seeker in order to qualify as a refugee: having 'a *well-founded fear* of being *persecuted* for reasons of *race, religion, nationality, membership of a particular social group* or *political opinion*, is outside the country of his nationality and is unable, or owing to such fear, is unwilling to avail himself of the protection of that country' (emphasis added). In its handbook first published in 1979, UNHCR stated that

> persons compelled to leave their country of origin as a result of international or national armed conflicts are not normally considered refugees under the 1951 Convention or Protocol. However, foreign invasion or occupation of all or part of a country can result – and occasionally has resulted – in persecution for one or more of the reasons enumerated in the 1951 Convention. (UNHCR 1979)

According to the UN Convention, persecution may occur in times of peace as well as in times of war, in situations of internal or international armed conflicts as well as in times of pre- or post-war tensions, during declared emergencies or because of repressive regimes. This means it is therefore erroneous to consider war or armed violence as the only legitimate ground for asylum. More generally, what this situation suggests is that the confusion over old and new forms of conflict and what constitutes a 'war' contribute to anti-immigrant attitudes, and to the culture of suspicion surrounding asylum claims.

In addition to this confusion around old and new conflicts, this chapter examines the impact of changing patterns of news consumption and uneven coverage of global conflicts on the repertoires of understanding available to media audiences in Italy and the UK. In a moment when the power and reach of European nations is shifting and the terms of mutuality in the international community are under question, the ways we understand conflict, international responsibility and interdependence impact directly on how migrants are viewed and received. Here we consider the framing of international conflict in the news and other media sources and the interplay between this media experience and attitudes to the role of European nations in a world of conflict and population movement.

Popular understandings of war in recent decades have been refracted through media representations, both the adventures and emotions of war movies and the changing framing of news reporting. Media do not only frame the understanding of reality: they have also become active participants and even catalysts in international crises and military interventions (Robinson 2002; Gilboa 2005; Seib 2008; Patrikarakos 2017). In the last twenty-five years, the narration and the fighting of wars has been affected by 24-hour news channels and live satellite broadcasts, constantly updated online news, blogs and other alternative sources of information, and social media such as Twitter and Facebook through which videos and pictures taken on phones can rapidly become viral. At the same time, ongoing declining trust in news outlets, accompanied with a far more fragmented, diverse and interactive media landscape than could have been imagined until recently, demands a revisiting of earlier certainties. We do not know *exactly* how media is interpreted by audiences (we have some broad understanding but we cannot anticipate the particular combinations of media examples or their interpretation by any particular audience member) and we do not know how *different* audiences put together their media use: practices of collating, assembling, sifting and cross-referencing are all developing at a rapid pace (Meijer and Kormelink, 2015). One aspect of this project has sought to plot some aspects of the diversity of media use in play today.

In order to capture something of the innovative strategies employed by younger, informed and technologically confident news audiences, we undertook a survey of university and college students in Italy and the UK. We focused on those studying programmes broadly in the fields of Humanities, Social Sciences and Media, including Journalism. In the survey, we asked about the frequency of news consumption, which news platforms were used and which forms of story were followed. This component allowed us to understand something of the changing news habits of younger, engaged audiences and, in particular, to register the use of multiple news sources and the sceptical reading that accompanies this form of news consumption. We also asked about coverage of global conflicts and their views on the responsibilities of European nations in relation to conflict and displaced populations. We necessarily surveyed only a limited population, focusing on younger media audiences, in order to map the range and manner of media use among emerging media audiences. We do not dispute that those who have always read printed newspapers and watched the evening television news may continue to do so. What we suggest is that this pattern of news consumption is likely to wane as the media habits of younger generations become more widespread. Whereas recent reports suggest that older audiences are more likely to share 'fake news' stories via social media (Hern 2019), our survey participants expressed distrust of news sources and alertness to partial and/or interested accounts. They were highly suspicious of mainstream media news. In this context of changing practices of media use, the purported power of the press to instigate hostility to migrants becomes uncertain, and other forms of media – such as social media, bear further consideration (discussed in chapter 3).

Histories of representing war

Our work emerges in response to the sense of uncertainty about the current meaning of war. What makes violence or conflict into a war? Which wars and uses of international force are defined as legitimate? Who or what is to blame? Thirty years on from the relative certainties of the Cold War, we are still searching for viable frameworks to make sense of what some scholars controversially called 'new wars' (Kalyvas 2001; Newman 2004; Kaldor 2012, 2013) and we have become accustomed to a proliferation of ever fragmenting conflicts. At the same time, non-state actors have become central players in the map of global conflict. We, the public, have become accustomed to new vocabularies of war, with an easy if anxious acceptance of the existence of smart weapons, asymmetrical warfare, collateral damage and, even international terrorism. These shifts in understanding are reflected in news coverage and consumption, with, ironically, the move to register civilian impacts militating against the inclusion of more analytic and contextual coverage.

The changing geography of warfare, with recent armed conflicts taking place overwhelmingly within civilian spaces, with predictably catastrophic consequences for civilian populations, has altered media repertoires of war reporting (for an account of the failure to register the legal implications of some recent military endeavours, see Nohrstedt and Ottosen, 2014). Mark Urban, a well-known BBC journalist, suggests there was a shift in news representations of the conflicts arising from the break-up of Yugoslavia:

> victimhood is everything in these conflicts and where it's almost impossible in the reporting of somewhere like Bosnia or Kosovo for someone with a gun in their hand to be a hero in the way that it was, even in the early days of the Northern Ireland conflict or the Falklands. (McLaughlin 2016: 51)

The larger argument being made here implies a shift in the framing of war. The uncertainties of the wars of the end of the twentieth century confused previous narratives of good and bad combatants. Understandably if predictably, wars in Europe were covered as human tragedies and, despite the vilification of some emergent popular villains such as Slobodan Milosevic, European audiences did not seem certain of which side 'we' were on. Who should we support in wars of multiple atrocities? Who, if anyone, could be seen to be fighting a just war? The difficulty of justifying military intervention is in part because recent and current wars impact disproportionately on civilian populations: residential areas become conflict zones, population displacement and ethnic violence become used as military techniques, and non-military casualties come to outnumber those of the formal military. We argue that these uncertainties, which characterise contemporary wars, raise challenges for audiences seeking to make sense of organised violence: warfare is going through a further phase of 'disenchantment' (Coker 2004). This disenchantment reflects a general discrediting of war and a significant decline in supposedly traditional military values of self-sacrifice, pursuit of glory and renown, in the eyes of society and soldiers alike. This disenchantment can fold into anti-elite populisms, with new movements to support 'our heroes' in the face of (perceived and actual) abandonment by the state and elites.

The news coverage of armed conflicts that shapes this apparent disenchantment with war, while simultaneously disguising ongoing military escapades, also reflects the political and technical reframing of war coverage. The changing landscape of war reporting is not only an outcome of new forms of war, it is also a reflection of increasing government awareness of the power of the media in conflict situations and resulting limitations on journalist access in zones of conflict. As the US withdrawal from Vietnam had been attributed by conservative circles to far too lax media coverage, with images of brutality, civilian victims and US casualties being blamed for changing public attitude to war, governments decided to apply innovative forms of restrictions on war reporting (Hallin, 1989). Referencing the experience of the war in Vietnam, the British government imposed tight controls on news coverage of the Falklands crisis, where only two photojournalists were permitted to enter the region and no television broadcasts were allowed (Harris 1983); the Reagan administration excluded the media from the opening phase of the invasion of Grenada (Hallin 1989). In these two cases, the war was covered exclusively by official sources. The military also became increasingly central as the fundamental source of information and perspective for journalists. After criticism of the resulting limitations of media coverage of US interventions, the Pentagon invented a new instrument for controlling war coverage: the so-called 'pool system', applied for the first time in the US invasion of Panama in December 1989. Highly dependent on the military for transportation and access to transmission facilities, journalists were not allowed to get into war zones if not a part of a 'pool': those trying to get into restricted areas were charged with 'breaking safety measures'.

The pool system was further developed in the first Gulf War, as journalists received specific guidelines on reporting and, for TV broadcasting, pictures and videos were provided by the military. Most of the images of war the public could see were the images of tanks, fighters, firing rocket batteries, images of precise smart bombs hitting the target, and images of highly professional soldiers who operated the machinery: through them only the military point of view was presented to the public. Interestingly, several commentators referred to the coverage of that war as a kind of 'advertisement' for the American arms industry (Griffin 2004). Some media experts described this form of war representation as 'Nintendo style' (Robins 1993). Analysing the virtual nature of this new war coverage, Jean Baudrillard (1991) provocatively claimed that 'the Gulf War did not take place', noting that the war existed more as a media event than a physical event. From this point of view, the first Gulf War has been paradigmatic as the US government created a new image of war: bloodless, surgical, waged by hyper-technological heroes. The public were denied access to representations showing the impact of war on human life: instead coverage consisted of images of hi-tech 'clean war', which satisfied the need for a zero-casualty use of military force. This video-game representation seemed designed to foster disengagement and distance among the public. Media coverage of this kind encouraged audiences to worry less about wars that appeared dehumanised, undertaken through technological means and distant from their lives (Huntermann, 2009; Mead, 2013).

In response to growing public scepticism about military interventions (Vietnam being paradigmatic of these failures) there have been attempts to re-enchant war through 'moralisation' (Habermas 2006), often supported by a revival of 'just war' theories (Walzer 1977; Orend 2006; Gentry and Eckert 2014). Media coverage of war has played a crucial role in providing a popular framing of military interventions as just and humanitarian within academic, military and government discourses. 'Humanitarian wars' (Roberts 1993), often euphemistically called 'humanitarian interventions' (Jahn 2012: 54), are military actions aimed at saving people in other countries from massive violations of human rights, primarily the right to life. What is at stake is not the protection of the state or of its own nationals abroad, but instead the nationals of third states, victims of internal violence sponsored by the government or by non-state entities. This doctrine seeks to extend the use of force by states in the case of flagrant violations of human rights. In the current legal framework, the combined right of victims to assistance and the right of the UN Security Council to authorise humanitarian intervention with military means do not amount to a 'right of humanitarian intervention' by states, individually or collectively. Indeed, the overwhelming majority of international lawyers consider that such a right cannot be recognised because it would violate the UN Charter's prohibition of the use of force.

The 1990s witnessed unprecedented levels of such 'humanitarian interventions': for example, the safe haven for the Kurds of Northern Iraq (1991), Somalia (1992–93), Bosnia (1992–95), the intervention of the Economic Community of West African States in Liberia (1990–96), the US-led intervention in Haiti (1994), French-led forces in Rwanda (1994), NATO's intervention in Serbia and Kosovo (1999), this last highly controversial as it occurred without legal authorisation by the UN Security Council. Humanitarian arguments demand a highly emotional representation of the suffering victims, able to solicit the moral obligation 'to do something', including the use of military force to provide protection and relief, and enforce human rights, freedom and democracy. The media attention on desperate civilian populations, however, is highly ambivalent and dependent on the frames of war coverage. In certain cases, such as in Rwanda, mainstream media reflected the sense of 'the West' as a compassionate yet distant observer to a conflict in which it could not, or would not, intervene. The choice to frame violence as an 'ethnic' or 'tribal' conflict, as a 'state of anarchy' or as 'carnage' instead of framing it as 'genocide' suggested that the targeting of civilians was the result of ethnic conflicts amongst 'backward populations' and has been critically assessed as contributing to non-intervention (Philo et al. 1998; Thompson 2007). In other cases, such as in Somalia, Bosnia or Kosovo, media attention to the victims has been supportive of military intervention, aimed to rescue innocent people from famine, genocide and 'chaos', by bringing material relief and protection while 'restoring hope', international peace and security (Roberts, 1999; Wheeler, 2000). In Italy, for instance, as a country with a rather muted or forgotten colonial past when compared to the UK or France, colonialism has been generally removed from national consciousness. In this context, framing military interventions as 'humanitarian' has been crucial for gaining popular support, while constructing the image of the Italian army as a 'force of peace-building in the world'.

In relation to news coverage of war/s, 'world system' frames are reinforced by journalistic conventions of coverage of violent conflicts. Frames of 'war journalism' (Galtung 2002) present conflicts as akin to a sporting arena where participants are grouped starkly into two opposing sides ('them vs. us') in a zero-sum game. This framing highlights the more visible effects of war, such as armed attacks, casualties and physical damage to property, while marginalising its less spectacular consequences. Our analysis of news coverage of twenty-first century conflicts showed that mainstream media in Italy and the UK omitted the historical, economic and political context for the reported events, failing to give voice to all actors, including the victims of war, or to report on peace-making initiatives. As a consequence, despite their spectacular and sensationalist tone, such reports add to audience uncertainty about the character and impact of conflicts. They reduce our imagined repertoire of international responses to the greater or 'smarter' use of force.

This context of uncertainty about the causes, direction and proper response to violent conflict raises questions about the manner in which popular support for military endeavours can be sought. Studies on the impact of war coverage on military decision-making suggest that only after governments turned their attention to the situation in the country did the media see events there as worthy of extensive coverage (Mermin 1997). It has been also noted that, in many cases, media attention for humanitarian crises increased only after Western troops were deployed in the region (Ogundimu and Fair 1997). Other analyses of media coverage argue that emotional responses to the story of the victims has deterred reporters from critical examination of the complex issues underlying a conflict (Burg and Shoup 2000). Moreover, not all humanitarian crises have become the target of intensive media coverage encouraging humanitarian interventions. As Walter Goodman remarked in an editorial on *The New York Times*,

> there is a disquieting aspect to the notion of policy being driven by images on the tube. The television camera is as blunt as it is powerful; *it is a prisoner of its own immediacy*. The pictures from Somalia cry out that *something must be done*, but they never help the viewer choose between doing something here and not there. *Why send troops to Somalia instead of to Mozambique, where as many or more people are at risk and the pictures are no less heartbreaking*? (Goodman 1992, emphasis added)

The second Iraq War (2003) was emblematic of attempts to frame military interventions as 'just war', including through the use of counter-terrorism arguments to justify intervention. The decision to wage war in Iraq was framed both as a response to international terrorism, and in terms of the 'right to pre-emptive self-defence', as was claimed by the Bush administration. The emphasis on *imminent* aggression legitimating the use of force is significant in terms of shifting the justification from responding to an imminent threat to a response to the *risk* of aggression. The 'war on terror' represents the paradigm of this kind of self-defensive war at global scale, in which 'the West' plays the role of victim of aggression by 'Islamic fundamentalism' within the general frame of a 'clash of civilizations' (Huntington 1996). Self-defence arguments demand an exaggerated representation of the enemy as evil and threatening, maximising the fear of the imminence and magnitude of their attack. The 'global terror' frame, for instance, is characterised by associating images of horror and brutality with non-state actors, which are put in opposition to the images of surgical precision and cleanness of Western hyper-technological war. Projected at a global level, this frame obscures local causes and dynamics for the diffusion of 'terrorist' groups which are assimilated, from Somalia to Nigeria to Afghanistan, to the same global network of Islamic terror.

The Iraq War is also significant here because – even more than previous wars – it was presented as entertainment. For example, the embedded reporting system deployed during the 2003 Iraq invasion relied on the pleasures of the extreme sports idiom for much of its effect. The system made for incredibly compelling television precisely because it provided a venue for the viewer to safely fantasise about entering the battlefield through the eyes of a fellow 'ordinary' civilian journalist (Stahl 2010: 17). This intensification of 'militainment' (Stahl 2010) involved the reframing of war coverage to appeal to audiences schooled in new viewpoints of sports coverage and the pleasures of approximating 'real-life' experiences. As Susan Sontag and Judith Butler have noted, the visual perspective that the military permits the media to represent actively structures our cognitive apprehension of war. This is a much subtler form of manipulation than censorship: 'restricting how any of us may see is not exactly the same as dictating a story line, it is a way of interpreting in advance what will and will not be included in the field of perception (Butler 2005a: 822).

Although such practices were designed to shape and manage audience reactions, our sense is that, far from cementing identification with a US/UK military project, embedding journalists has, over time, confirmed a global scepticism towards the justification and conduct of war. The military's intention was to enhance the reporters' credibility by enabling them to be at the scene of hostilities themselves, and simultaneously to reassert the deterrent force of modern American arms and the impression of the army's invulnerability. This new form of war journalism became possible thanks to the new digital transfer mode systems, which allow real-time broadcasting of reports directly from the fields, a technological shift that enabled new forms of rolling spectacle (Mirzoeff 2012). Initially US journalists supported such processes of embedding, relieved that the restrictive information policy of the Afghanistan war had ended. However, more recently, doubts have emerged about the impact of such a close and dependent relationship with the military on the credibility of news reports.

Questions about the legitimacy of 'just wars' should be seen within the wider context of distrust of official accounts and public institutions, interwoven with an increasingly vocal distrust of mainstream media. This quickly became another central theme of our research, prompted by the extreme scepticism voiced by survey respondents and the rapid emergence of debates about fake news, political disengagement and the symbiotic relationship between populism and distrust. Ironically, the cautionary tale of Western adventurism was linked in our survey responses to more recently popularised modes of war reporting. As we discuss in relation to our survey responses later in this chapter, the presentation of the valiant Western forces and an overly celebratory account of their exploits was itself a trigger for distrust of the mainstream media among those we surveyed.

Changing frameworks of war

The background to this confusion, distrust and reinterpretation is the transformation of the terms, practices and techniques of warfare. Popular media has schooled audiences to understand war as a particular kind of narrative, with the suffering or heroism of 'Western' forces presented as a focal point. The shift to 'new wars' (Kaldor 2012) as the only mode of armed conflict has transformed global understandings of conflict, with battlefields indistinguishable from civilian spaces, and increasing confusion between the statuses of combatant and civilian, most markedly in the identification of legitimate targets for violence.

Despite all we have learned of the diffusion of combat space, mainstream media continue to present conflict zones as delimited areas. Occasionally we are encouraged to support interventions to remove civilian populations from the line of fighting – and this is presented as humanitarianism. However, when we are forced to recognise that there are no spaces beyond the war for anyone and no fantasies of safe havens or delimited zones of conflict, our narrative repertoire runs thin. In effect, and despite the seemingly endless appetite for bloody and triumphalist representations of war, European audiences have very little access to the events of war on the ground (Hawkins 2011).

Narratives of war in representations of refugees

Narratives of war play a crucial role within coverage of asylum. Refugees are imagined, first and foremost, as the products of organised and armed violence. In some cases, violent conflicts previously silenced by mainstream media have received wider public attention only after they produced a significant number of displaced people, the level of attention often being proportionate to the proximity and number of potential asylum seekers to European borders. For instance, according to many analyses, the image of

Alan Kurdi's drowned body on the Turkish beach produced a significant and sudden interest in the war in Syria (El-Enany 2016; Mortensen, Allan and Peters 2017; Slovic et al. 2017).

Narratives of war are intrinsic to the legal framework governing both asylum claims and the extent to which countries are deemed safe to return. War narratives also shape public attitudes and media representations in relation to asylum seekers. The extent of public sympathy and solidarity may depend on the different representations of war or conflict in the countries that people have left. It is evident, for instance, that discourses which delegitimise asylum claims produce suspicion and hostility. In our research (discussed in chapter 3) we came across assertions that people are not fleeing any war, or that their country is safe, or that they had passed through a safe country, or that they are really terrorists disguised as asylum seekers. Discourses of this kind delegitimate refugees, helping to convert them into 'illegal' and 'deportable' migrants; they also create cynicism and distrust towards the asylum process and the organisations involved. Such assertions also aim to extend sovereign power to select those who cross national borders, while suspending principles and rules of asylum.

There are in fact differences and even contradictions between 'primary' narratives of war, which concern the direct representation and understanding of violent conflicts as such, and 'secondary' narratives of war, which evoke violent conflicts only indirectly as the main cause for people displacement and asylum issues (Lambert and Farrell 2010). In the news these two narratives are generally treated as separate because they respond to different political purposes: as we have demonstrated, primary narratives of war aim to justify the involvement of Western armies in violent conflicts abroad; secondary narratives of war, as we will show below, aim rather to undermine Western responsibilities and obligations toward people on the move.

These primary war narratives encompass new forms of conflicts, typical of the post-Cold War era, while secondary narratives of war seem frozen in older accounts of conflicts (Lambert and Farrell 2010). This is hardly surprising if one considers that the Refugee Convention, which still provides the point of reference for international asylum law, was established in the first years of the Cold War and from a Eurocentric perspective (Chimni 1998). This is why it framed the archetypical image of 'the refugee' as an individual, rather than a mass of people, 'fleeing oppressive, totalitarian, and particularly Communist government' (Loescher 2001: 44) because of violations of civil and political rights, rather than social and economic rights. At the time, the prototypical agents of persecution were authoritarian states rather than armed non-state or sub-state entities. As a result, those displaced by the conflicts of recent decades often do not fit easily into the terms laid out in the Convention.

War, information, entertainment, nation

We have mapped out this background in order to show the points of connection between media depictions of war and the utilisation of this media coverage by political actors seeking to disallow asylum and other forms of migration. To continue this analysis, in this section we present findings from the survey we carried out with 212 young people in the UK and Italy. We sought to understand how young people gathered and made sense of news about global events. In particular, we asked about the role of media representations in informing audience knowledge and understanding of the conflicts in countries from which significant numbers of asylum seekers and migrants come. We distributed an online survey on audience use of news media to young people in Italy and the UK. We understood that news media has been undergoing a period of rapid change, in terms of the proliferation of platforms and changing formats, including among established news providers.

Our survey included questions about frequency of news consumption and, importantly, news sources which were used. This allowed us to understand the expanded terrain of news media that is informing and influencing contemporary audiences. We also included questions about attitudes to international responsibility and law as well as understandings of the causes and consequences of violent conflict. We used these responses to help us understand how views of conflict and our responsibilities towards those impacted by conflict are formed. Although our sample was not large, we felt that the voices of these emerging media users illuminate the rapidly changing patterns of news consumption that shape contemporary opinion. This matter deserves further and more extensive study. Here, we use results from our survey to put together an account of how audiences construct an understanding of a world of unpredictable global events in an era of distrust of mainstream media and official accounts.

The advent of continuous media and of instantaneous transnational transmission has transformed the place of news within a larger media formation (Thussu, 2008). Whereas rolling news gives a sense of being constantly informed and appears, superficially, to increase the volume of information and the extent of popular access, it also contributes to the shift towards news as entertainment. The emergence of alternative media platforms presents the opportunity for different understandings of global conflict, including through sharing access to citizen-accounts that come together in a crowd-sourced version of non-expert war reporting.

When framing our research, we had guessed that those accessing news through new media formats might absorb a changed set of news values, with celebrity/scandal/conspiracy displacing more established topics of high news value, such as war or international politics (Theocharis and Quintelier 2016; Wood, Corbett and Flinders 2016). Yet, despite the proliferation of information sources and the merging with other genres of entertainment, respondents in the UK showed that 'war and conflict' definitively remains the main issue followed in the news (85 of 112). Respondents in Italy identified 'war and conflict' as the second most followed issue in the news (68 of 100), preceded by 'immigration' (70 of 100). The Italian result is probably the effect of the long-term intense media coverage of events related to search and rescue operations in the Mediterranean, especially after the Lampedusa shipwreck of 3 October 2013 and of the beginning of the *Mare Nostrum* mission (Carta di Roma 2015; Carta di Roma 2017).

There is little sign here of a turning away from the mainstream news agenda. However, the manner in which respondents described their news consumption reveals the complexity of interpretation embedded in everyday infotainment practices (Fletcher and Nielsen 2018). Many responses showed a keenness to demonstrate that respondents were not duped by media companies. In retrospect, it is apparent that the survey was viewed by young people in education as a test of their knowingness and they, dutifully, explained that they did not believe everything they read or saw.

Somewhat unexpectedly, these proclamations of knowingness continued to imply that objective news coverage was possible. Despite the recognition of differing interests shaping news outputs, our survey showed that younger media users continue to strive to find accurate information, often through labour-intensive and wide-ranging sifting of media reports. One gives an insight into this approach by saying, 'News is produced and written by people. I do believe there is "objective" news which is really accurate.'

The organising term of objectivity is important here. A recurring theme among our respondents was a concern about media 'bias'. The term 'bias' itself indicates a belief in a pre-existing or underlying 'truth' that is contaminated by 'bias' but, nevertheless, exists somewhere alongside or within interested and misleading accounts. This framing can be seen in the various accounts of active investigative news consumption that arose:

> Readers must understand all news sources hold a bias, you should look at multiple sources to get a good idea of news.

> It depends on which media outlet you mainly use, although the BBC is debatably bias, its one of the most reliable sources we have

> despite being funded by the government – some newspapers e.g. the sun are extremely biased towards a particular political ideology and therefore shouldn't be trusted. (UK)

The strong desire to demonstrate knowingness, critical awareness and a healthy and absolutely expected distrust of mass media could be attributed to this sample and their recruitment (our survey was distributed through colleges and universities). This gives rise to a tension in responses. On the one hand, respondents wished to identify and critique the power of mass media forms. On the other, they were keen to show that they themselves were not fooled. We will consider the impact of this performative consumption of news in later chapters.

This framing of bias makes sense only against a presumed objectivity that pre-exists or exists outside the biased representations. However, critical audiences are able to discern the existence and degree of bias and it is this awareness that allows news consumption to continue to be meaningful. Some responses suggested that it was impossible to imagine a 'bias-free' form of news, but that people still considered some things to be 'facts' or 'good sources':

> All news is biased, even if based on fact.

> All sources are biased, in different ways, so a plurality is necessary to counterbalance this. Ultimately no news media is ever going to deliver the authentic truth in the fullest extent but you can get a general idea of context from a few good sources.

Our survey was distributed during a period of increasing debate about so-called fake news. As most of our respondents described their media use as focused on online sources, it is unsurprising that their responses show considerable engagement with these debates about trustworthy sources and the modes of informed reading. Substantial proportions detailed their own reading strategies of combining and comparing multiple sources, seeking to further verify information relating to controversial topics and looking to alternative news providers as a corrective to mainstream news forms.

Strategies of cautious reading included:

- Varying techniques of interpretation according to the topic of news items, with some 'controversial of political' stories demanding greater skepticism:

> I mostly trust the information if the issue reported is not controversial or political, otherwise I take care trusting it.

- Approaching all news sources as flawed and employing a system of story-checking among a number of sources:

> I read knowing that there may be bias, so I tend to look to see what other media sources have said about the issue as well before forming an opinion.

- Distinguishing between hard facts, outright lies and partial accounts, with the suggestion that news media could be trusted to provide some hard facts but within a context of limited reporting:

> Media is always going to be biased, although facts and figures may be correct they often will not tell the whole story.

- Most of all, our respondents professed a certain amount of pride in not being taken in by flawed news media. This knowing distrust pervaded answers, sometimes with an element of exasperation, as if this was too obvious to mention:

> Have to take all Media with a pinch of salt.

Although our responses revealed complex interpretative tactics in relation to consumption of news, they also showed awareness of the dangers that could arise from generalised distrust of news reporting:

> By and large, I do trust the media to provide accurate information; I genuinely dislike conspiracy theorists, who keep questioning every

> single bit of information and who are often revisionist on even the most established of facts (such as the Sandy Hook mass shooting deniers or Holocaust deniers); that said, I am, however, aware that every media outlet has a certain angle and bias, so what I do is to consult many different newspapers and outlets in order to get a fuller and more nuanced picture of what is going on, and this also provides some sort of fact checking mechanism.

This comment reveals the wider context of suspicious and tactical news consumption, while also pointing to the dangers unleashed by what they term 'revisionism'. A similar, if less explicit, view was expressed by a number of our survey respondents. While seeking to demonstrate their credentials as knowing and sceptical audiences, a role enacted through the cross-checking information and the practice of consuming multiple news sources in order to 'cancel out' the distortions of any one outlet, our respondents retained a strong belief in the importance and relevance of news coverage. Despite all of their many comments on 'bias', they agreed, largely, that there was a truth out there and also that this truth could be uncovered through these practices of discerning reading.

For our survey respondents, one important reason for their ambivalence or distrust towards the media was that they felt it did not sufficiently inform them about international relations, conflicts, wars, and migrations or provide enough contextual information to understand these kinds of global events. Respondents felt they had limited access to information relating to conflicts regarded as beyond the interests of Western nations. When asked which conflicts they were aware of, our respondents in the UK said they knew about countries where wars had taken place including Syria (15.2%), Iraq (14.4%) and Afghanistan (13.7%) but only 2.4% knew about conflicts in Eritrea. As for the Italian respondents, they felt informed about wars and conflicts in Syria (94%), Libya (69%), Iraq (57%) and Afghanistan (56%) but only a few about Eritrea (8%). Elsewhere in this book we consider the absences in mainstream media (and schooling) in relation to some regions of the world and the imperial histories of Western nations. Absences confound the attempts of discerning audiences to uncover truths through practices of triangulation.

Although many of our respondents were aware of a number of wars and conflicts, they felt media did not provide them with adequate frameworks for understanding them. Asked if they felt news media helped them to understand the background and context of conflicts in the world, 42.7% of UK respondents said yes, 30.9% said no and 26.4% answered they were not sure. In Italy numbers of those who answered yes or no were much closer, respectively 35.6% and 34.7%, while 29.7% answered they were not sure. When asked to explain their negative or uncertain responses, comments frequently referred to lack of clarity (in certain cases a lack of credibility), as well as a lack of detailed information and deeper analyses of events, as in the comments below. One respondent explicitly referred to the national focus of news and the lack of journalists on the ground as limiting the usefulness of media in understanding conflicts around the world.

> Too often news media tend to hide the real aims of wars.

> As conflicts are complex phenomena, it is almost impossible for a news article to cover them exhaustively. Moreover, each country tries to minimise or hide its role in those conflicts, with the result that news media do not go very much in depth.

> News media do not talk very much about what happens abroad. They are more interested in the eventual consequences on Italy.

Some respondents considered these limitations as structural to mainstream news media, stressing the need to consult books, specialist magazines and websites in order to receive a much more complete and nuanced analysis of conflicts, as in the following comments:

> News present some facts or events. Understanding conflicts is a much more complex operation, which cannot rely on media news only.

> For the understanding of some issues, such as wars, books are much more useful.

In response to a further question, concerning the aspects of conflicts that media helped them to understand, Italian respondents identified the location (92%), the protagonists (69%) and effects of the conflicts in terms of people's displacements (64%). UK respondents provided very similar answers, as they felt the media helped them to understand where conflicts are happening (91%), who is involved in the conflicts (75%) and how people are displaced by conflicts (62%).[1] This suggests that the media is useful in registering certain areas of the world as conflict zones from which people are forced to leave, but it is unclear how much the media is useful in developing an analysis of the context.

Awareness of the media's limited contribution to the understanding of international relations and conflicts becomes evident in the following responses to the question 'How does news coverage of global conflicts make you feel?' UK respondents complained about the narrow focus of much news coverage:

> Some inform you a lot, some only focus on how it affects us in Britain despite it happening thousands of miles away, making me feel slightly angry.

> I often feel that I'm being given a very specific account, and without being given the context of the conflict I feel like I'm being deliberately left in the dark about most aspects of the conflict.

In a context where news functions as entertaining spectacle, coverage of war and conflict also functions by appealing to emotions. It is unsurprising, therefore, that our respondents described heightened emotional responses arising from media coverage of international conflicts:

> [I feel] Compassionate, upset, angry, motivated to do something to help.

> [I feel] Disheartened, sad, angry.

Nevertheless, as another respondent noted, contemporary coverage of wars is strongly reminiscent of fictional forms, making it difficult for audiences to assess the material they are presented with:

> [I feel] alienated. It doesn't seem real, as though the events happening outside are fictional.

Our respondents spoke of the disconcerting impact of the continuum between entertainment and news, influenced by the advent of 24-hour news channels and of instantaneous transnational transmission. Whereas rolling news gives a sense of being constantly informed and superficially seems to increase the volume of information and the extent of popular access, rolling news also contributes to the shift towards news as entertainment. The techniques of 'militainment' (Stahl, 2010), resulting from the embedding of the media and the prevalence of a military, highly technological and 'clean' representation of war, may contribute to this unsettling sensation of distance or unreality.

One respondent, for instance, mentioned a jingoistic and militarist tendency (holding the British Armed Forces on a pedestal) which has parallels with the compulsory patriotism flagged up by US authors in relation to the post-911 climate (Achter 2008; Gray, Jones and Thompson 2009); they say they find this distressing:

> Often is quite distressing, depending on how the coverage is presented, tabloid press in the UK for example almost hold the British Armed forces on a pedestal, nearly infallible. Plus the triumphalist tone often taken like with the infamous 'Gotcha!'

Italian respondents also expressed very mixed feelings when asked about the impact of news reporting on wars and conflicts. This ranged from fear, frustration, sadness and indignation, to emotional distance and indifference. This was expressed within the following comments, some of which denounce the objectification of suffering and spectacularising wars as a form of 'pornography' or expressing concern about the confusion between fiction and reality.

> Limited and distant. This is how I feel actually.

> Media let you live in the 'its-happening-now' dimension, which is decontextualised from deeper and real causes. This produces that moment of commotion (in the case of dramatic events) in connection with a confusion on the reasons why this actually happened.

> I feel part of a world addicted and indifferent to war and terror.

> You have the impression you're watching a movie. News coverage lacks real empathy.

UK respondents also flagged up lack of context and explanations for the causes of conflicts:

> It's never full coverage, some aspects are insisted upon, while leaving most aspects (influence, perpetrators etc) in shadow.

The lack of context, combined with the partial and narrow Western or national focus of coverage, caused respondents to feel helpless and confused, as in these further UK responses to 'how does new coverage of global conflicts make you feel?':

> Haunted. Disheartened. Sad. Worried.

We had a number of one-word responses to this question of emotional response, including 'Angry', 'Disheartened' and 'Depressed, tbh'. After the earlier detailed discussions of critical media use and the need to contextualise the partial and interested accounts of Western media, the admission of upset is saddening. Although one person explained the sensation as 'sad, but glad to be aware', most dropped any celebration of being 'well-informed' when asked directly about how coverage of conflict made them feel. However many sources were assembled and cross-checked, knowing did not make things any better. Instead,

> [I feel] helpless. War seems constant.
>
> [I feel] often frustrated. Poor coverage of facts and speculation do not help attitudes. Also tired, over time people naturally become apathetic to suffering.

With this final quote, the respondent cautions that people can become indifferent in conditions of information overload, particularly when they have limited energy and attention ('also tired'). Ironically, in the absence of historical and political context, the move towards human interest-focused stories may exacerbate a sense of disconnection and helplessness amongst audiences. In particular, this limited audience attempts to identify responsibility or to call for greater accountability. Without a framework to make sense of global politics, there is a sense that certain regions of the world are perpetually at war and that war is something like a natural disaster, without specific actors and geopolitical causes. At worst, media coverage could convey that human suffering was unavoidable, as unpredictable and unstoppable as the weather (Kyriakidou 2015; Doboš 2019).

Moreover, bearing in mind the 'worlding' of news coverage, our respondents are observing and responding to a situation where mainstream news coverage does little to map the global interconnections between Western countries and other parts of the world, or to explain how countries are linked through legacies of colonialism or foreign intervention, or through neo-colonial global inequalities, instead perpetuating what some have called 'colonial unknowing' (Vimalassery, Pegues and Goldstein 2017). As a result, war and repressive regimes appear as phenomena which have always existed and continue to exist elsewhere, and for which Western countries bear no responsibility. The responses above suggest an awareness of the limitations of this perspective.

Respondents were also concerned about the dangers of rejecting global inter-connectedness, as in their responses to the question 'What concerns you most about global conflicts?' Comments from both UK and Italian respondents suggested that despite dominant media representations which present people outside the West as distant 'others', global conflicts might be closer than we might think and might pose an immediate threat to Europe:

> Although no war has happened in Europe I fear it could spread soon enough, and with recent developments such as the appointment of president-elect Trump and Brexit, the so called traditionally 'big' states are undertaking in controversial policies, therefore I think conflict is near unfortunately. And with the vertical and horizontal proliferation of nuclear weapons such as the renewing of Trident, I don't see a positive future for us. (UK)

> They describe wars as something always distant, as if we were protected from the possibility to be directly involved in armed conflicts in the coming future. (Italy)

> That European nations are too weak to assist with conflicts, or have exacerbated problems with their involvement. The retreat away from 'world government' (e.g. Brexit) is worrying. (UK)

> The rise of the far-right using conflict to advance their agendas, i.e. manipulating fear of outsiders. (UK)

> My family or friends' safety. (UK and Italy)

The comments by Italian respondents stressed the destructive potential of arms (particularly nuclear weapons), the high number of deaths including civilian deaths, the fear of terrorism and the development of those conflicts into a 'Third World War'. They also expressed fears about the endlessness of wars:

> Nobody is really looking for solutions.

> I'm scared by the unaccountability and the indifference of decision-makers, who could do something [to end conflicts].

They also expressed concern about increasing isolationism, nationalism and mistrust of international institutions, in connection with the rise of right populism within Western nations:

> This lack of a true international understanding and framing of conflicts, which is not new, goes hand in hand with a revival of nationalisms. (Italy)

> The rise of nationalism and so less international co-operation, leading to more competition and conflict. (UK)

> National-interest and rise of populism. (UK)

UK respondents also mentioned fear of terrorism:

> Increased threat of terrorism (when the Middle East is concerned). Potential Economic troubles depending on where the conflict is taking place. Increased amount of migrants.

> Terrorist acts within our borders.

Following on from this sense of impotence in the face of global events, there is a larger sense, especially among UK respondents, of being helpless. In particular, the rise of right populism is seen to be an inevitable and unstoppable global force, against which individuals can do little.

We asked our two samples to identify the main repercussions of international conflict for European nations. In Italy, perhaps in response to the larger influx of people during the refugee crisis, by far the most frequent answers were related to the displacement of people and rising numbers of asylum seekers (48 out of 83). This was often framed as inevitable but not necessarily negative for Italy or Europe, sometimes accompanied by criticism of the European failures in the management of the 'migration crisis'. Besides generic answers on growing instability, insecurity and fear, the second most frequent answers were related to terrorism. Some respondents ironically affirmed that conflicts may have positive effects on the European economy because of the flourishing arms industry.

In the UK, of the 78 that offered a further response, 24 felt that greater numbers of migrants and refugees was a major repercussion of international conflict for European nations. Eight named the threat of terrorism. The majority of these comments were neutral or supportive of the rights of refugees. However, displaced populations were regarded as among the most visible and tangible impacts of war for European societies. A number of comments made it clear that refugees were considered to be one symptom in a wider formation:

> In a globalised world, I think, international conflict has repercussions on European nations, such as economic repercussions, stronger influx of immigrants who flee violent conflict zones, and political repercussions, such as the current rise in right-wing and nationalistic politics and movements across Europe.

Further answers in the UK expressed country-specific concerns, reflecting the time the survey was distributed:

> Countries decide to leave the EU (Brexit) because of refugees coming in – or immigrants in general. This weakens the EU.

> Refugee Crisis. Brexit. Donald Trump.

One reflection of the timing of our project is the repeated return to Brexit, with 10 from 112 responses mentioning Brexit explicitly. At the same time, 22 of 112 UK respondents mentioned Trump or the US election. Together, Trump and Brexit have created a renewed engagement with news media. Arguably, the Trump campaign and his subsequent election have transformed global news consumption, signalling a break with the technocratic presentation of neoliberal politics. Instead of faceless, nameless institutional actors behaving in seemingly impenetrable manners, Trump returns political coverage to matters of character, drama and humour. Despite the incredulity of the world, the day-to-day business of US government has become a matter of global mass news coverage (Boczkowski and Papacharissi 2018).

Some UK participants stressed also the ongoing dilemma of whether or not to get directly involved in conflicts, such as Syria, where UK military planes had been deployed against Isis in the so-called 'Operation Shader' since September 2014:

> To intervene or not. Send troops and lose lives and face backlash or stay out watch the situation deteriorate and face backlash.

> Dead troops and bad media. No-one wants war, and yet if we don't go to war it is shunned as not helping.

Across the project, participants revealed or critiqued the tensions between Western ideals and the impact of the actions of Western nations. This tension could be identified alongside concerns about excessive numbers of refugees coming to Europe.

> Guilty conscience that we have played a part in the deaths of many. Financial strain in accepting refugees. Inability to have European ideals accepted worldwide.

This rapid movement between guilt and concern, to concern and resentment, to concern and disappointment and disillusionment typifies the overall structure of our responses.

Central to this work is the question of how media accounts of conflict frame other political questions, including the question of the rights of migrants. Our project was conducted through the period of Brexit campaigning, referendum and the initial stages of negotiating the terms of leaving. This meant that, in one sense at least, the question of national sovereignty was highlighted in public debate and news media and a great deal of popular energy devoted to discussing the importance or otherwise of a particularly frozen account of sovereignty. Within this debate, the right to determine borders took on a much more amplified place than the right to military defence, but the two aspects of imagined sovereignty did work together in Brexit logics (Bachmann and Sidaway 2016).

Asked about their personal responsibility to victims of conflict, in the UK the majority of respondents showed a keenness to express helpful attitudes, by supporting welcoming activities, combating prejudice, raising awareness about conflicts and displacements, raising money for supporting international aid, and campaigning for human rights. Other respondents expressed contradictory points of view, in order to express their distress towards asylum seekers coming to the UK:

> [My responsibility to victims of conflicts is] to vote for parties that will not let them in by the hundreds of thousands. To vote for a party that will control the borders of this country while at the same time sending aid to those victims, in the region and refugee camps. To not use sob stories to aid ISIS in getting their soldiers into our countries. To donate to charities helping in the area of the conflict.

Further respondents refused any individual responsibility, some asserting that they were not 'responsible for colonialism', others expressing a sense of powerlessness:

> It's hard to know, as the media mostly represents the issues with victims of conflict, not what we can do as individuals.

In Italy, a significant share of respondents (25 out of 82 who answered the question) stated that they did not feel any personal responsibility towards people displaced by war and conflicts. This may be in relation to the ambiguous and de-contextualised ways in which Italian media usually represent 'boat people' and everyday rescue and disembarkation operations. People on the move are represented simultaneously as passive victims and as a potential threat to the national economy, security and cohesion. However, rescue operations and asylum issues are represented as a closed and highly specialised system, in which there is no place for individual human solidarity or volunteering In some cases, personal responsibility and involvement may have been discouraged, as rescue and asylum issues have been presented in the public debate as a 'shady business', as we will show in our discussion of the anti-NGO campaign which has inflamed Italy since 2016 (discussed in chapter 3).

Some respondents, however, tried to contest the victimisation and criminalisation of displaced people, stressing the importance of recognising the agency of asylum seekers:

> [We should] look at people fleeing war as our peers, as people with agency, not through the simplistic stereotype of the victims.

> [We should] go back to consider them as human beings, not just numbers which create problems.

Conclusion: back to war and politics

As we assembled the final version of this work, echoes of the Cold War had returned to British news media. The mysterious and deeply unsettling poisoning of the Skripals, a Russian father and daughter in Salisbury, unleashed a plethora of Cold War tropes. From the explicit disruption of the terms of diplomacy, through the tit-for-tat expulsions of diplomats, to the demands for solidarity from 'allies', this set of events was narrated as a going back to a politics of war that we could understand.

There are some obvious ironies here. While on the one hand, the attack came to be read as a sign of resurgent Russian aggression, on the other, British media continued to include little or no coverage of Ukraine or the ongoing war there. The nations that were reported as rallying around in solidarity with the UK represented an earlier phase of global alliances. Emerging/emerged economies did not figure in these accounts. The Global South as a whole remained out of view. The US was, slightly belatedly, brought on side as confirmation of the continuing relevance of NATO. Unlike the uncertain terms of engagement in the war on terror, the Salisbury attacks appeared to constitute a familiar and frightening encroachment on a sovereign nation. After decades of unfamiliar terms, this appeared as an old-fashioned act of war and, it seems, the British media public has been alarmed by the prospect of a return to a Cold War style framing of global politics.

Against this backdrop of a rapidly reshaping configuration of global politics, the partial and uneven coverage of global events positions European media audiences as innocent victims in a changing and dangerous world. Both the forgetting of historical connections and the under-reporting of contextual factors contributes to this sense of victimhood – because 'we' are uninvolved, 'innocent', minding our own business and it is 'they' who are impinging on 'our' world. In this changing landscape of apparently unpredictable risks, the movement of displaced and often desperate people is framed as another threat against beleagered European lifestyles. Mainstream media depictions of conflict and its consequences seem designed to produce not only confusion but also cluelessness. The active erasure of historical links between Europe and other parts of the world adds to the bemusement. Unsurprisingly, European media audiences have little opportunity to comprehend who these 'others' are – to each other or to us – or to grasp the circumstances that lead to their displacement. Even when empathy is made possible, perhaps by the humanising impulse of a liberal media and/or an audience shaped by the values of humanitarianism, what is needed to achieve global justice appears beyond our imaginations. In response, and as so many of our survey respondents say, we may feel pained and/or gloomy but still have no clue of what is to be done.

In our work with those displaced by conflict, there was clear exasperation with European historical amnesia, but this was not a call for greater education in the name of tolerance. Although we have been interested in the factors that shape attitudes to 'migrants', we have tried to use these insights to uncover the making of a 'Western' subject, to reveal the shifting construction of this shadowy creature who must be forever implied in any making of 'migrants' but who is so rarely seen. Our displaced respondents were angry or upset, and occasionally amused, at their treatment in Britain and Italy – but their response was not to call for greater tolerance. Instead, they made us understand that they were claiming no more than their rights. For this to be understood in Europe, European audiences needed to relearn their connections with the rest of the world and comprehend the complex mesh of culpability and interdependence that sews us together. Without this, justice will remain unimaginable.

Notes

1 Note that respondents could choose more than one answer, leading to totals of more than 100%.

Interlude 2

Songs, jokes, movies and other diversions

This interlude will explore the conversations we had with migrants in the UK and Italy about fun and entertainment. Speaking to migrants about fun and entertainment may seem counterintuitive from the perspective of mainstream media coverage, in which migrants are rarely asked about anything other than their migration journey, which frequently involves testimonials of hardship. However, this reduces the role of migrants to one-dimensional figures of heroic suffering. Also, participants had experienced quite considerable difficulties both through fleeing other countries and dealing with the asylum system. Because of this, asking about fun or entertainment felt like an awkward and counter-intuitive thing to do. Fun and entertainment also seemed like trivial topics given the hardships our participants had experienced, and because of the pressures on them to present themselves as suffering, and therefore as deserving.

Despite the awkwardness, we felt that asking participants about fun and entertainment was a way to provide some insights into the complexity of their lives, challenging what is often a one-dimensional representation of their experiences. Humour also emerged in the discussions as a form of social solidarity for our participants: it enabled them to laugh at Home Office officials and others who had power over them, and to share jokes with each other. Crucially, humour and entertainment also played a role in developing an alternative analysis that challenged dominant readings of global conflicts and the immigration system (particularly in relation to legacies of colonialism). In this section, we will discuss some of the examples that refugees in Birmingham, Nottingham and London shared with us, including songs, jokes and comedy clips shared on social media.

Music and films as an imaginative resource

We asked participants if there was music they associated with their experience in the UK, or which gave them some sense of hope in the face of the circumstances they were dealing with. Some of them mentioned music from the countries they had left, or shared YouTube clips with us. This included Nubian music from Sudan, Kurdish music from Turkey, as well as Nigerian gospel music. Some of the music they shared also had explicit political messaging. One participant, a former politician with the African National Congress (ANC) in South Africa, shared YouTube clips of community songs. One of them was composed by exiled ANC politicians in Zambia under the Apartheid regime. She shared the lyrics:

One day we will come back home (repeat)
There will be thunder
Some will cry
There will be fireworks

Describing one of the songs in an email, she said, 'they sang the song with hope because at that time Nelson Mandela was sentenced to life in prison. Nobody knew that he would be released one day but their hope never died' (email correspondence, 2 March 2017). Another song was also composed under the Apartheid regime, and had an explicit anti-colonial and anti-racist message:

We as a Black nation
We are crying for our land
That was taken by the whites
Let them leave our land

In the conversations we had in person and over email, she brought this anti-racist and anti-colonial analysis to her experiences of the asylum system, as well as the lack of understanding about Africa she saw in Britain. Although the song was composed in a different time and context, the memories of her involvement in that struggle had some resonance for the situation she was currently facing.

Others mentioned songs and musical genres that had become significant to them since coming to the UK, and which did not have any obvious connection to the countries they had left (also raising questions about our assumptions about refugees' cultural consumption habits as always referring back to the country of origin). For example, another participant described how 'Talkin' Bout a Revolution' by American folksinger Tracy Chapman resonated with the struggles he faced in the UK, particularly poverty and unemployment:

> I listened to a lot of … the soundtrack at that time for me was Tracy Chapman, Revolution song, you know, because of the odd little jobs I did as well I felt like … you know when she talks about 'waiting in the welfare line'. Because there was a time when I didn't have a job and I had to do the dole and everything. I'm not an emotional weepy kind of personality but if there was ever a song that draws me close to tears it's Tracy Chapman's Revolution song. (London, 1 April 2017)

In this case, a song which was composed in another time and context became an imaginative resource for surviving poverty and thinking about social justice.

For others, entertainment provided a sense of release and escape in the face of very difficult circumstances. One participant mentioned how gospel music comforted her and gave her 'stress relief' (Nottingham, 19 April 2017). Another respondent from Nigeria now living in Nottingham mentioned becoming a fan of Bollywood, out of a desire for something different from either British or Nigerian culture.

> Shah Rukh Khan, Akshay Kumar, Priya Chopra. I watch a lot of Bollywood, I don't watch any other. I used to watch American, but

> I just stopped British and Nigeria movies; I just stopped … I will call a friend; please can you help me record this. I do Bollywood. I just like them, their singing, their culture. Let me get something different from my own culture. (Nottingham, 19 April 2017)

As an escapist film genre, Bollywood can provide a sense of release for those in a very stressful situation; it also is not loaded with connotations of either the culture she has left or the culture of the country where she is trying to make her life. The availability of Bollywood films could potentially reflect the cultural landscape of where the location is based (the Midlands) and the presence and legacy of the South Asian community there. More generally, it could reflect the globalisation of Bollywood beyond South Asian audiences.

Comedy

Comedy was a frequent reference point. This included satirical animated programmes such as *South Park* and *Family Guy* (London, 1 April 2017). News comedy programmes such as those hosted by John Oliver, Jimmy Kimmel, Samantha Bee, Trevor Noah and Stephen Colbert, were popular with some participants.

> Oh and I watch a lot of these, so that's Stephen Colbert, he's a satire comedian … Yes, so I watch a lot of satire comedy. Trevor Noah is one of my favourites. Jimmy Kimmel, yes Jimmy Kimmel, what's his name, Bill … Maher or Moher or whatever. Stephen Colbert, Seth Meyers, who else, Samantha Bee, her. So I've been following the story in the States because of this, because that's what they talk about a lot and it just makes me laugh and in a way, it's not just making me laugh but I'm listening to what is going [on].' (Nottingham, 19 April 2017)

News comedy provided a way for the refugees to inform themselves on current events, but also to provided them with some sense of release ('it makes me laugh'). For some, it also functioned as an imaginative resource to develop an alternative analysis on global politics. To varying degrees, the comedians the participant mentioned are known for their critical perspectives on American and international news, in some cases perspectives which are absent from mainstream news media.

Laughing at power

This was also the case in the stand-up comedy sketches which some of our participants shared with us as video clips on WhatsApp. One of these was a sketch by South African comedian Trevor Noah on the John Bishop show called 'UK Border Agency' (2015), in which he tries to explain to a suspicious border official when entering the UK, who thinks he is lying and is up to no good, that he is a comedian ('So you're a comedian? You don't look funny. Do you have any jokes?'). Noah flips this logic in order to draw parallels with the history of colonialism in Africa – whereby the British claimed to be there with benevolent intentions but were there for other reasons. Another clip, an episode from *The Daily Show* (2015) juxtaposed quotes from US President Donald Trump with remarkably similar quotes from infamous African dictators including Idi Amin, Muammar Gaddafi and Robert Mugabe.

How to understand these responses? There are many different interpretations of both humour and laughter; in *The Philosophy of Laughter and Humour* (1987 cited in Critchley 2002), John Morreall classifies them in three different ways. The first involves humour provoking feelings of superiority over others (as represented by the thought of Plato, Aristotle and later by Hobbes on humour); second, 'relief theory', where laughter involves the discharge of psychic energy which would be normally used to repress the unconscious, which emerged in the nineteenth century through the work of Herbert Spencer and later by Freud; and third, 'incongruity theory', in which humour is produced by an incongruity between the situation at hand and common-sense expectations and knowledge, which was developed first by Francis Hutcheson in *Reflections Upon Laughter* (1750), and explored further by others later on.

The comment that 'It just makes me laugh' suggests a sense of release. As mentioned, the migrants we interviewed were faced with such difficult life situations that any sense of release at all was very important. Furthermore, the comedy examples described or shared with us can also be understood in terms of incongruity: specifically revealing the absurdity of global geopolitics and an immigration system which makes it so easy for some to cross borders and so difficult for others. Revealing the absurdity of border regimes opens up questions about global inequalities, racial hierarchies and the ignorance resulting from colonial legacies. To use the example of the Trevor Noah sketches, why is it seen as so inconceivable for South Africans to travel to the UK for comedy shows, or for dictators to hold power in wealthy Western countries? As Simon Critchley points out in *On Humour*, 'by laughing at power, we expose its contingency, we realise that what appeared to be fixed and oppressive is in fact the emperor's new clothes, and just the sort of thing that should be mocked and ridiculed' (2002: 11). Laughing at power can be an important resource for developing a critical analysis of the situation, and also points towards the possibility that the situation could be different.

Another way in which participants laughed at power was through pointing out double standards, and the challenges this posed to global inequalities, racialisation and ignorance. The critique of double standards was present in an internet meme shared with us through WhatsApp, which compared two newspaper stories about the boxer Anthony Joshua. Joshua was described as a 'son of Nigerian parents' when he was arrested for possessing cannabis, but as a 'British boxer' when he began to win fights. It was also present in the aptly named *Double Standard*, a spoof newspaper the participants in Nottingham put together (discussed later in this book), which raised questions about how borders were closed for many people but open for major corporations, including those which produced environmental and social damage in the countries they had left.

This critique also served as the basis of a joke shared with us in an interview, which makes fun of colonial ignorance:

> I remember at one time when I went to another school to teach, they said what language do you speak, can you speak in African? I said to them, look, there's not a language called African. Africa is a continent with multiple languages. Which exactly did you want me to speak? And also, there was this joke that was circulating then that all white people think Africa is a country, its capital city is Nigeria and its president is Nelson Mandela. (London, 15 March 2017)

These jokes were a way of laughing at colonial ignorance that they encountered on an everyday basis.

Humour as social solidarity

Humour was also a way of creating social solidarity, often in the face of what could be extremely stressful situations. In the UK, asylum seekers are required to sign at an immigration reporting centre. Signing was a frightening experience for many of our participants, as sometimes people would be arrested and sent to detention centres with no warning; their phones would be taken away so they could not contact anyone (including their solicitors). One participant described how she and others at the reporting centre had identified a particular immigration official who was recognisable because of being visibly overweight, and who had a particular reputation for harshness. They would joke about whose turn it was to get the 'big lady':

> There's this big lady that everybody is scared of, so we always hope when you get the ticket that you don't go to her because you can feel really intimidated ... So we always say, oh, I'm going there then I'm going to get that big lady there and then we always laugh about it. (Birmingham, 24 February 2017)

Laughing together about who will 'get that big lady' is a way that people help each other feel less alone in a situation which is meant to isolate and intimidate them, with their fates in the hands of often unsympathetic immigration officials.

The examples we have described are about what can be learnt from experiences that are normally considered to be trivial diversions, particularly in relation to the testimonials of suffering which are normally expected from migrants, and from the hardships of the asylum system discussed elsewhere in this book. However, we feel the songs, jokes and comedy clips are important because of how they provide imaginative resources, both for survival under very challenging circumstances, and also – crucially – for developing an alternative analysis of global inequality, racism and legacies of colonialism – and particularly as they relate to the asylum system. The limitations of the mainstream media coverage discussed earlier makes them particularly important to consider.

3

Social media, mutual aid and solidarity movements as a response to institutional breakdown

Introduction

Earlier in this book, we discussed media coverage of wars, and international relations more generally, and how this produces a sense of helplessness, confusion and general distrust for media audiences. Information about global conflicts seems inadequate, biased, and does not give people enough of a conceptual framework to understand or respond. This is connected to a sense that international and national governments are failing to deal with global conflicts, meaning that wars seem endless and unresolvable, and that states are involved primarily for self-interested reasons. This sense of confusion and lack of agency may also be a dimension of media audiencehood. In *Seeing Things* (2000), John Ellis proposed that television brought in a generalised mode of witnessing in which there was little agency, meaning that audiences obtain a 'powerless knowledge and complicity' (2000: 1). He slightly revised this position in 2009; however, he still argued that mediated witnessing is marked by both emotional ambivalence (knowing *what* you feel without knowing *how* to feel) (Ellis 2009a), and a sense of scepticism and incredulity (Ellis 2009b: 76). In 'Photography, Journalism and Trauma', Barbie Zelizer argues that mainstream media representations of atrocity (such as the wars in Cambodia, Bosnia and Rwanda) did not involve public witnessing as was the case with the Holocaust, but instead presented iconic images of extreme forms of suffering (Zelizer 2011: 61). Instead of inviting identification and empathy, iconic images of suffering (which have since become the norm) allow the viewer to adopt a position of voyeuristic fascination or emotional disengagement (Zelizer cited in Meek 2010).

In chapter 2 we discussed how these conditions created distrust in migration governance. This chapter explores responses to this distrust in the media and the government. These responses are very much about ad-hoc tactics of 'making do' (de Certeau 2011: 29) for the sharing of information, and in some cases mutual support, in the face of limited information and the systematic failures discussed earlier. Within this context, social media platforms are frequently used both as an alternative news platform and as an organising tool. In the absence of accessible, legal means for people to seek protection, migrants and their supporters were left to rely on platforms such as Facebook or WhatsApp – in some cases literally for their lives, with the indices of the sharing economy as the only measure of trustworthiness. Social media platforms have been controversial recently for their role in data mining, fake news and undermining democratic processes. They are also owned by Silicon Valley tech giants, which are not publicly accountable. This reveals the fundamental *ambivalence* of the internet and particularly social media platforms, as Whitney Phillips and Ryan Milner have argued (2017). Social media platforms can facilitate mutual aid networks, practical solidarity and alternative perspectives, but as will be seen later in the chapter, can simultaneously function as conduits for bigotry and hatred.

Central to this chapter are ways in which migrants dealing with the asylum process (who are those at the sharpest end of the system) share information and facilitate mutual support in response to an immigration system which seems impenetrable, arcane and cruel. We also examine how they use the news in the countries they have left (particularly where the news was censored, such as in Zimbabwe, or where little media coverage exists, such as in Afghanistan). We will then discuss how support groups in the UK and Italy use social media platforms to organise practical solidarity for those who have fallen through the cracks of the asylum system, provide updates on a rapidly changing situation (as in Baobab Experience and Presidio, the two solidarity groups in Italy we studied, discussed in detail later on). Social media platforms are used by solidarity groups to produce alternative media, as well as to reframe or critically comment on mainstream media coverage of refugee issues. Finally, we discuss the responses of anti-migrant groups, and particularly how they share conspiratorial narratives about the ugly truth of immigration and lend them a degree of credibility and authenticity not possible within mainstream news contexts.

Following the news in a climate of censorship and limited information

In our interviews with migrants in the UK and Italy, we asked how they used media and news outlets to inform themselves about developments in the countries they had left, and the countries where they were currently living. We found that similar issues emerged around distrust of the media, as experienced by the survey respondents, but also that they were dealing with a situation where access to news was quite limited, and where the technologies which would enable access to the news had become politicised. In the UK, asylum seekers have restricted access to television and the internet. They live in housing which was once managed by local authorities but has been outsourced to private security companies such as G4S and Serco. As one participant told us, there are no televisions allowed in asylum housing, due to controversies around this as a perceived luxury item, which makes it difficult to follow the news (Nottingham, 19 April 2017). Living on the £37.75/week allocated to asylum seekers also makes it difficult to afford mobile data, limiting how much news can be accessed on phones. This means that news can be often consumed in a fragmentary manner, and that refugees are often reliant on networks of friends, family, and diaspora networks.

In Italy these structural obstacles to accessing news did not exist, as accommodation centres generally provide free wi-fi. Those needing access to the internet outside the accommodation centres used part of their daily allowance to purchase mobile data. However, in certain cities, asylum seekers were housed in hotels without free wi-fi, which provoked protests. This situation both demonstrates the importance of internet access for those in the asylum system, but also its politicisation as demands for free wi-fi provoked sarcastic and sometimes hostile responses from right-wing local politicians or newspaper commentators, who saw this as evidence of the 'insatiable character' of asylum seekers, who came to live off the public purse wanting the 'good life' without doing anything all day long (see chapter 4 on the construction of the figure of the migrant). The use of mobile phones amongst African asylum seekers in Italy also became a flashpoint for local newspapers to stoke public anger and outrage around smartphones and tablets as perceived luxury items and symbols of disengagement. For example, there were allegations that that people who possessed smartphones could not be possibly be fleeing war (as discussed, it was assumed that people could only seek protection if they were fleeing war). Refugees were also criticised for 'always being on their phones', implying rudeness and lack of integration with Italian society. This reflects some contradictions around the perceptions of the internet and mobile technologies as promoting either democratic engagement or disengagement. Moral panics around smartphones as undeserved luxuries have notably become a widespread trope in media coverage since 2015. Examples of this include stereotypes of young people as hedonistic consumers of information and communication technologies (ICT) and dismissals of Syrian refugees who use smartphones and take selfies (Leurs 2017). As Koen Leurs and Sandra Ponzanesi have observed, the image of digitally connected refugees does not fit with dominant Eurocentric ideas of passive, suffering, 'sad and poor refugees fleeing war and atrocities' (2018) and perceptions that migrants and refugees are not the intended users of ICTs (Leurs 2017).

The participants in our project discussed challenges they faced in accessing the news in the countries they had left, due to difficulties in accessing news generally, and the lack of international media coverage (as discussed in chapter 2), but also in many cases due to the media censorship in these countries, meaning there was little mainstream coverage of currents events there. In response, they often sought news through personal contacts in the countries they had left. For example, one UK participant (a university lecturer from Sudan in Birmingham) mentioned getting information from Sudanese politicians as well as through the British Consulate in Sudan (Birmingham, 16 February 2017). An Afghani participant in Italy also reflected on the methods he used to find out the news in his country of origin, and the limitations of traditional news media in providing a full picture of the situation on the ground:

> I use the phone also to reach some news pages, read what my friends in the country post, and follow the situation on the ground in Afghanistan. Sometimes I also read some news in Italian newspapers on the country, after a terrorist attack which killed tens of people. Not all news are given, you know, especially not those concerning certain regions. In order to really understand what is going on in your city or village, you have to ask some of your friends or family members who still live there. (Pisa, 10 April 2017)

In addition to seeking the news through personal contacts, social media was also useful. For example, one UK participant emphasised the importance of social media as a platform for citizen journalism:

> Like there were YouTube videos where they were demonstrating about the Gukurahundi,[1] which happened in Zimbabwe and we lost our relatives there. And Facebook now, there is this thing now, you call it self-reporting. Similar on YouTube, or Facebook. The thing on Facebook where you record yourself, and come up, talk, recording people when they are talking as well. (Birmingham, 3 April 2017)

A participant from Zambia mentioned checking YouTube to keep up with the news in his country saying that 'I'm always going back to finding out if there's any changes in the area of freedom of speech' (Birmingham, 2 February 2017). Another (an exiled politician from South Africa) mentioned watching the South African Parliament on YouTube (Birmingham, 24 February 2017). However, while social media proved useful, our respondents also expressed concerns expressed about the limitations and risks of social media, particularly within the context of authoritarian regimes, as exemplified by the experiences of a Kurdish human rights activist from Turkey, now living in the UK:

> I used Facebook, against, like, Erdoğan for six, seven years, but they shut it down all the time. I hate Facebook as well, honestly. As a human rights activist, you can't go on because they shut you down and because Erdoğan, he's got people, like trolls. (Birmingham, 10 March 2017)

There were also concerns that active participation on social media might draw unnecessary attention and therefore affect the status of asylum claims. For example, when asked about his level of participation on social media, one participant (a migrant from Afghanistan now living in Italy) added:

> I generally do not post or comment too much on political issues on Facebook. I still don't feel comfortable in doing this. Maybe after I receive a permit to stay and will be able to move free in Europe. (Pisa, 10 April 2017)

There was a sense that too much social media participation would make one too visible, potentially leading to immigration application being refused.

Mutual aid processes for navigating the asylum system

Migrants in both the UK and Italy were dealing with an immigration system which they found confusing, frightening and arbitrary in terms of the decision-making. Official guidance was bureaucratic at best and completely incomprehensible at worst, particularly for those who were struggling with English or Italian and had limited access to legal advice. Mutual support and information sharing therefore became vital, particularly from friends or relatives who had successfully claimed asylum and established themselves in the new country. WhatsApp, Facebook and other social media platforms were used to facilitate mutual aid systems. For example, one UK participant mentioned belonging to a WhatsApp group including people who 'have been through the system', who shared information and advice about claiming asylum (Nottingham, 19 April 2017). Articles shared through Facebook or other social media platforms also proved useful in offering a rich source of unofficial insider knowledge from those with successful asylum claims. This was particularly important when preparing for the interview which would ultimately decide the success or failure of the claim. For example, a participant from Afghanistan mentioned receiving advice from his cousin about 'how to behave' in the interview:

> Via WhatsApp I asked a cousin of mine, who already received the residence permit, how to behave during the interview, what to tell the commission, how to present my story. He sent to me one or two news articles describing the current situation of violence in our region of origin, to support my claim. I also asked other friends to give me further details about the asylum demand and what to do in case of rejection, as the [Italian] law recently changed. Many of them sent me news articles in English. They were not easy, but they helped me to better understand what the lawyer of the centre said to me when we met. (Bologna, 28 March 2017)

In the absence of clear and accessible legal advice and what seemed like hidden agendas in the asylum system, WhatsApp groups and other social media platforms provided unofficial information and mutual support. Such information and contacts were all the more crucial for those travelling to Europe via clandestine routes (which should be understood as desperate measures in the absence of accessible legal means of travel). Within these situations, they only had each other to rely on. For example, a participant from Nigeria told us about the crucial importance of using social media for mutual support in coming to Italy, as they could not even trust the person who was taking them there:

> We all used Facebook, Messenger or WhatsApp very often during our journey, and will for sure continue to do so, if we decide to leave Italy. Accessing GPS through mobiles is crucial during the trip. Once, we used this system to find out that smugglers were bringing us in a different direction than agreed before. Information you can get through the web or through Facebook pages is also very helpful for deciding where to go and how to get there. We used mobile phones also to call the Italian coast guard to be rescued, when we were on the boat in the Mediterranean. (Pisa, 28 March 2017)

An Afghani participant in Italy also told us about how the journey to Europe was arranged on Facebook – with all the risks that this involved. The only way of determining credibility was through seeing how many Facebook friends the smuggler had on the personal page (the assumption being that someone who was not trustworthy would have few friends).

> When I arrived in Izmir, a Syrian friend I just met there showed me on his smartphone that on Facebook there are quite hundreds of pages of 'smugglers', offering their services, with full contact numbers! It was easy to contact some of them, although it was difficult to tell which services were safe and which were not, and how much you had to pay for the trip. He told me that smugglers are on Facebook also with personal pages: those who have been active for several years now have over 3,000–4,000 friends. He picked up one of them to get in Greece. (Pisa, 10 April 2017)

Within such clandestine contexts, the sharing economy (as represented by the number of 'likes') becomes the only way of gauging trustworthiness, particularly when dealing with strangers. This raises questions about the role of social media and the sharing economy in such desperate situations where there are no other means of guaranteeing safety; in the absence of state support or networks of friends and family, people are forced to rely on corporate platforms, which are only accountable to their shareholders.

Beyond the sharing of information and mutual support, migrants were also beginning to organise around their conditions and how they were being treated. For example, one Eritrean activist in Italy (who became a point of reference for fellow Eritreans on the move to Europe) used social media as a platform to publicly condemn the detention and exploitation of migrants in Libya (many of who are Eritreans). Videos were published on YouTube documenting protests in detention centres. After these news and videos were circulated to a larger public on Facebook, around 200 have apparently been released (*Avvenire*, 7 August 2018).

These mutual support networks were also used to share information and warn others about racism and anti-immigrant sentiment, in the context of rising xenophobia in the UK and Italy. For example, a participant from Mali told us what he knew about protests going on in Italy against reception centres for asylum seekers:

> I usually use Facebook to talk with friends who are still in Mali or in other European countries. Other times, I use it just for killing time, like I use YouTube for videos and music. Sometimes I discuss with friends also about politics, about the situation there, or the problems that we face here. We comment privately on some videos seen on some online newspapers, or some article on *Jeune Afrique*. One of my closest friends once heard in an African news broadcast about protests against accommodation centres for asylum seekers in Italy, and asked me for further details. You know, there is often news in our national TV channels trying to discourage young people from moving. I didn't hear about these protests against African migrants, but then I found some news about it on the internet – it was an Italian newspaper – with the help of my Italian teacher. She translated the most difficult parts of the article. I was disappointed. I started worrying about similar protests against my centre too. (Pisa, 28 March 2017)

Within situations where access to information can be limited and fragmentary, these networks for sharing information can be vital. This is particularly important in the multilingual, transnational context in which migrants often operate.

Migrant support networks: mutual aid in the face of state breakdown

If the migrants we interviewed in the UK and Italy had to rely on informal support networks for news and advice about navigating the immigration system, then this was also the case for solidarity groups in both countries. These groups were often in the position of providing volunteer support in the absence of state provision (or, as discussed earlier, its politicisation), and providing alternatives to counter a hostile media climate. We studied two pro-migrant Facebook groups/pages in the UK and two in Italy, and four crowdfunding campaigns in the UK on the JustGiving Platform. We explored the way in which these groups developed practical responses to the situation, as well as their attempts to produce alternative interpretations. Facebook was a key vehicle for disseminating information, mobilising and organising people, and collecting resources. In order to get a sense of these grassroots initiatives and popular understandings, we focused on networks that were led and coordinated by volunteers rather than by established NGOs, political parties and campaigns. We chose Facebook rather than Twitter because we wanted to explore the interpersonal relationships between posters, and we wanted to explore bottom-up perspectives rather than from the 10–20% of accounts which tend to hold disproportionate influence within Twitter networks (Meraz and Papacharissi 2016 cited in Siapera et al. 2018).

Our analysis captured the posts and comments within three snapshots. The first period was September to November 2015, in order to capture the initial response to the Alan Kurdi photo which provoked such a strong media reaction and what was, in retrospect, a temporary shift in public opinion towards a more empathic attitude to asylum seekers. The second was May to July 2016, in order to explore integration of asylum seekers into UK and Italian societies, when more people began to arrive and were no longer perceived as 'distant others', and when 'moral panic' spread after Paris and Brussels terrorist attacks. The third period was September to November 2016, to examine how the situation developed, and any shifts in public opinion.

In Italy, we used Netvizz, a data collection and extraction application, which enabled us to identify pro- and anti-immigrant Facebook groups through keyword searches. The two most popular pro- and anti-refugee groups were selected. Notably, the most popular anti-immigrant Facebook page, 'Stop Clandstini' (50,000 members) was removed after being reported to Facebook for racist content. In the UK, a different approach was taken. One of the researchers was added to a local refugee solidarity Facebook page by an activist contact; a second page was identified through cross-posting, and the anti-refugee group through keyword searches.

In Italy, the two Facebook pages that we studied were:

- Baobab Experience (BE), a Facebook page opened on 19 June 2015, liked by 43,091 people and followed by 43,394 people (as of 9 August 2018). When we started monitoring this page, on 20 June 2015, 33,707 persons were already following it.
- Presidio Permanente No Borders – Ventimiglia (NOB), a Facebook page created on 15 June 2015, liked by 14,583 people and followed by 14,455 (as of 9 August 2018). When we started monitoring this page, on 20 June 2015, 14,639 people were following it.

In the UK, the Facebook groups that we studied were:

- West Midlands Solidarity with Refugees (WMSR), a Facebook group with 646 members based in the West Midlands, which arranged for donations and other practical support for refugees in Calais in 2015 (most of the group's activity ceased after this point).
- Refugees at Home (RAH), a Facebook account of a small charity with 9,676 followers and 9,534 likes (as of 10 November 2018),

and which matched refugees with local volunteers who would host refugees in their homes.

In addition, we looked at a number of crowdfunding campaigns in the UK on the JustGiving platform, focusing on those with the greatest number of contributors:

- 'Makers for Refugees' was a group of 96 online businesses who raised £9,011 for the Red Cross.
- 'The Syria Refugee Pub Quiz' raised £432 via ten supporters through a pub quiz on 15 September 2015, which was donated to CAF-UNHCR.
- 'Crowdfunding to buy urgent supplies for refugees in Calais' raised £2,000 with 27 supporters making Zakat or Sadaqah donations during Ramadan.
- 'Raising £1,000 to welcome Syrian families across West Kent by supplying essentials to assist their new start in life' involved 65 supporters camping for a night on local farm land and raised £1,515.

Both the initiatives in the UK and Italy were trying to provide emergency support which both the state and the voluntary sector had failed to provide. On their website, BE define themselves as 'a group of volunteers and private citizens that, in 2015, found itself facing a migratory emergency of about 35,000 migrants passing through the walls of our Baobab Centre [an occupied, social space], located on Via Cupa, in Rome [near Roma Tiburtina Rail Station]'. They provided food, clothing, emergency accommodation, healthcare assistance, psychological support, legal assistance, and spaces for leisure and rest.

After receiving a police control order on 26 November 2015, motivated by anti-terrorist and security concerns in the aftermath of the attacks in Paris, on 6 December the social centre was forcibly evicted by the centre-left Municipality. The official motivation for the eviction was the pressure on the municipal administration by the owner of the occupied space to have it back in his control (*Corriere della Sera*, 6 December 2015). After the eviction, volunteers continued their support activities in street camps. This was supported by a growing network of human right activists, and medical and legal associations, engaged both at the national and European level, and by people living nearby. Significantly, no requests for government or EU funds were requested or provided, in order to maintain a degree of independence from the state.

At the time of writing, over 70,000 people have been hosted through BE, with at least 300 people welcomed per day during the busiest periods. Some of them are trying to reach Northern Italy or other European countries after first entering Europe in Sicily. These people typically stay no longer than two or three days. Others supported by BE are destitute and are waiting to enter the asylum process and to be assigned places in accommodation centres. This unique experience has resonated among activists, public figures, and artists, both locally and internationally.

As the volunteers declare on their webpage, their initiative is a clear response to institutional breakdown: 'Our experience at Baobab proved that the city of Rome has a strong and aware civil society, which responds with promptness and humanity when institutions seem to only show indifference' (Baobab Experience). Despite the growing networking and organisational effort, the grass-roots dimension is crucial to its identity:

> Baobab Experience is a constantly evolving thing: everyone can become a volunteer or supporter and take part in this experience, by providing some time to help, by donating cloths and other needed materials, by subscribing or supporting our fundraising campaign.

Volunteers characterise their involvement in BE as a basic act of humanity: 'in the absence of institutional action, no one should look at the despair of other human beings without taking action'. They deliberately reject the more restrictive environment of formal reception centres in Italy, meaning that everyone can have access to Baobab, offering time, support and skills.

From the beginning, BE volunteers used their Facebook page to share news and information, mobilise people, and put out calls for support. Posts included many requests for specific items, such as shoes, backpacks, suitcases, medicines or food. They also created a specific page for food deliveries. The most recurrent posts reported daily on the centre followed by a list of what was needed (food, shoes, cloths, tents, medicine etc.). These functioned as a series of press releases, in order to keep both supporters and the general public informed. These posts became much more dramatic when the centre was forcibly evicted by the police and the Municipality of Rome failed to find alternative spaces for hosting their activities. During the eviction, the Facebook page was used to document police and institutional behaviours towards the centre, its hosts and initiatives.

During the eviction, the Facebook page was used to document the actions of the police and the state towards the centre and the people involved with it through images, short videos and interviews and comments. Despite the emotionally charged character of the subject matter, the posts were sober and descriptive and did not include images of people in distress, instead documenting tents and personal objects destroyed in the eviction. Communications focused on the dubious rationale behind the decision of the Municipality to evict the centre and the lack of support for people who had become homeless as a result of the eviction. The threats of deportation and the coercive behaviour towards the hosts (including forcing them to present identification) were denounced as violations of human rights.

Refugee solidarity campaigns in the UK had a similar practical orientation, particularly in terms of providing support that was otherwise lacking. The photograph of Alan Kurdi washed up on a Turkish beach in early September 2015 came to stand for the human cost of anti-refugee rhetoric and policies. Many felt that the cruel, intolerant and mean-spirited mindset did not represent them, but they also felt that – given the intransigence of the government and what they felt were very prevalent anti-immigrant views – that they would have limited success in lobbying government and changing policy. The only way of making a difference, therefore, was through practical support activities such as donating clothing or other necessities, or funding charities supporting refugees; at least this would help individuals if larger structural changes were not possible.

The Facebook group members rarely discussed the causes of the refugee crisis, if at all. For WMSR and RAH, it was assumed that group members already knew the causes of the refugee crisis already and that there was a pro-migrant consensus, meaning there was no need for further discussion. There seemed to be little evidence of trolling (although the pages were moderated), possibly because participants were like-minded and the page was not visible enough to be targeted by the far-right. Discussions in WMSR and RAH werw almost entirely concerned with arranging practical support. For WMSR, this primarily concerned the collection and transportation of donations, which was particularly challenging in rural communities. The organisation sending the donations to Calais (the Amirah Foundation) seemed quite disorganised and difficult to contact. Group members had very limited information about what was needed, and so they were left guessing about what donations were required. This gave many of the discussions the awkward character of strangers speculating and guessing about what was needed and how they could help. Posts also linked to crowdfunding campaigns to purchase essential items and donate money to charities such as CalAid and Doctors of the World. Much of the discussion on RAH was dedicated to the practicalities of pairing hosts with guests, and the practicalities of arranging this. The crowdfunding campaigns also had a similar practical orientation, including arranging donations of emergency foil blankets, wool blankets, tinned food, rice and oil. The campaign was set up during Ramadan and was encouraging people to donate money as Zakat or Sadaqah. It was organised by Muhammad Elsawy, who described himself as brought up in London by Egyptian parents, highlighting the role of diaspora communities in these initiatives.

There was a sense that for WMSR and the crowdfunding campaigns, refugees were imagined as being somewhere else: Calais,

Kos or, in some cases, elsewhere in Europe, although a few posts also referenced support groups for refugees who were already in the UK. This was also the case for the crowdfunding campaigns, which were largely about sending donations to other places, as in 'Crowdfunding to buy supplies for refugees in Calais', which raised money to buy supplies for refugees in Calais, Dunkirk and Paris, or 'The Syrian Refugee Pub Quiz', which donated money to UNHCR. 'Raising £1,000 to welcome Syrian families across West Kent' was about supporting refugees in the UK. However, it mobilised the symbolism of refugee camps in other parts of the world, as it involved sleeping in a tent for one night.

Both the Facebook groups and the crowdfunding campaigns were about goodwill and voluntary labour as a stopgap for the failings of minimal or non-existent state provision due to both austerity cuts and the politicisation of refugee support. Many of the migrants supported by RAH had fallen through the cracks of the system: they had recently claimed asylum and were waiting to be allocated housing, or they had recently been granted refugee status and their benefits were immediately withdrawn (including housing), meaning they were temporarily homeless. One of the crowdfunding campaigns, 'Raising £1,000 to welcome Syrian families across West Kent', was also focused on providing necessities to refugees, and, in particular, covering shortfalls in the Syrian Vulnerable Persons Relocation Scheme. The campaign also involved an acknowledgement of relative privilege compared to those seeking protection, as exemplified by the description included the following statement:

> for those of us in the leafy South East of England, the idea of 'camping' most likely prompts thoughts of fun and adventure. We may have early memories of camping out in our gardens as excited youngsters, or maybe later on in our lives of camping out at music festivals, or of walking holidays in the hills and mountains. ('Raising £1,000 to welcome Syrian families across West Kent 2017)

The statement above seemed to reflect some of the more dominant liberal humanitarian discourses often seen in the mainstream media as well as by the 'thin solidarities' (Turner and Rojek 2001) characteristic of many humanitarian charity campaigns. Like the other crowdfunding campaigns, it was a one-off event. However, in the discussion about how camping means different things to different people, there is at least an acknowledgement of global inequality, which is often absent within similar campaigns.

Positive messages to counter official negativity

Beyond offering practical support, the campaign groups challenged mainstream discourses around the 'refugee crisis', framing refugees either as a problem, or as helpless victims. For example, a short post published on BE's Facebook page on 2 September 2015 read: 'Today at Baobab 437 meals have been distributed. No numbers on the arms. Just welcoming activities and many other things which let our friends smile again and be serene'. The post implicitly referred to reports from several international and national newspapers about authorities in the Czech Republic who wrote numbers on the hands and arms of 200 (mostly Syrian) migrants at Breclav railway station. The act of writing numbers on human bodies evoked disturbing memories of the Nazi era, provoking protests from human rights advocates and Jewish organisations.

For BE, other recurrent posts, especially in the first period of the sample, published simple testimonies of people volunteering at the Baobab Centre. Sharing accounts of welcoming asylum seekers on the Facebook page can be understood as a way of reflecting on experiences and encouraging solidarity actions. For example, Francesca (a doctor and volunteer) posted about her experience of treating a young migrant with a high fever. After a while he should have felt better, so he left the ambulance without saying a word. She looked afterwards for him everywhere, as she was worried about him. When they finally met in another common room of the centre, the young man simply hugged her and said 'thank you, mum Africa'. The final lines contained the core message of the post: 'that night my heart was fuelled by a great joy … I'm the one who has to thank you, boy. Because love for one's fellow people overcomes every barrier, be it linguistic, cultural or religious' (3 September 2015).

A similar post (7 September 2015) recounted the experience of Giulia, who had just accompanied a Sudanese boy to the station with his parents and two sisters, who were travelling to Munich. The poster used the incident to discuss the media construction of the refugee crisis. She couldn't help but contrast the happy ending of the Sudanese family's story with the tragic end of Alan Kurdi, whose image had circulated worldwide some days before. 'A cruel picture and a solidarity turn' was the title of this post, in which Giulia bitterly commented on the power of Alan's image, anticipating that sympathy and openness will not last long (which, in retrospect, turned out to be the case).

> The death of Alan, coldly documented and obsessively spread, has been necessary for making European leaders change their attitudes: Ms. Merkel now opens the borders, while earning the nickname of patron saint of refugees and enjoying the honour of her photos exposed as holy pictures in many rail stations. Bavarians who welcome Syrians in Munich by singing 'Ode to Joy'[2]; Finnish Prime Minister who offers his holiday house to escaping migrants; wanting not to be outdone, even Pope Francis urges people to welcome refugees: every parish, a family, grand hotel style.

In the UK, the overall tone of both WMSR and RAH was also determinedly positive, as group members tried hard to encourage each other in a difficult climate. Members seemed aware they held unpopular minority views, particularly in response to public opinion, which was widely perceived as hardening towards immigrants. Two periods in the sample coincided with both the Brexit vote and the election of Donald Trump as US President. Group members seemed demoralised by these events, but saw the practical support they were giving to refugees as providing hope. For example, the day after Trump was elected, the following post affirmed faith in small acts of solidarity:

> Need to cheer yourself up this morning? Want to do something positive? Maybe we can't affect geo-politics or turn the clock back but we can help individuals. (9 November 2016)

The discussion by supporters of the crowdfunding campaigns were also quite upbeat (although this is unsurprising given the nature of these campaigns and platforms), with many supporters praising the initiatives.

The positive tone of the discussions was not only about mutual encouragement; it was about trying to project a different image of Britain – even if only to individual asylum seekers – from the official messages of hard-heartedness and hostility from the media and the government.

Protest actions

One of the groups in Italy, 'Presidio Permanente No Borders' (NOB), which operates in and around Ventimiglia, the Italian municipality on the Riviera close to the southern Italian-French border, took a more militant approach beyond the practical solidarity offered by the other groups discussed earlier. The city has been a place of transit between Italy and France for generations. In the 1930s, Jewish families in Italy used trails through the woods to flee the country. More recently, thousands of people – primarily from Sudan, Eritrea and Ethiopia, but also from Somalia, Syria and Palestine – have passed through this area in the hope of reaching France after crossing Italy. For many, the goal is to get to Calais, and then to the UK. But the journey has become increasingly risky because of the de facto closure of the border.

In the spring of 2015, the French government decided to reinstate the border between France and Italy. This decision has resulted in the blocking of thousands of people in transit (at least 15,000 each year) by French authorities. For example, all trains from Italy now stop in the Menton-Garavan railway station before entering France. People who look visibly 'African' are racially profiled and asked for documents in train carriages, toilets, waiting rooms or on the tracks, and are forced to return to Italy if unable to provide the necessary documentation. Cars, lorries and vans approaching the Italian-French border are monitored and frequently stopped and searched by French police officers, who then deliberately arrest 'African-looking' drivers or passengers. On 11 June 2015, local activists mobilised in solidarity with a group of (mostly Eritrean) migrants protesting against the decision of the French government to reinstate border controls with Italy, and then moved onto the rocks near the border in order to resist identification and eviction by the police. In June 2015 after the first protest, an informal settlement was established at the border. Tensions grew between the Italian police and the municipality, eventually resulting in the eviction of the camp on 30 September. From the beginning, NOB used their Facebook page to post daily updates of the situation on the ground, and to call out for support when the risk of eviction by police became evident: 'SOS. Everyone to the rocks of Ventimiglia for resistance' (30 September 2015).

In Spring 2016, the Italian government's strategy became more aggressive towards migrants who found themselves stranded in Ventimiglia trying to cross the border. For example, Angelino Alfano, Italy's former Interior Minister, pledged that 'Ventimiglia will not be our Calais'. By this statement, he expressed the government intention to avoid the building of a large migrant shanty town in Ventimiglia, close to the Italian-French border. By 'Calais', he was referring to the camp famously known as the Jungle, near the Port of Calais and the Eurotunnel used by migrants to travel to the UK. Since then, at least 4,000 people have been removed from the area, caught after being returned to Italy by French police, or during raids. Dozens of Italian activists, who had supported the occupants in Ventimiglia's informal camps, also received *foglio di via* – a controversial preventative policing tool that effectively bans them from the city for several years. During the same period, an ordinance forbidding members of the public from giving food and water to migrants was reinstated (it was introduced in summer 2015 but had been revoked in the spring). In an industrial area several kilometres from the town centre, a heavily policed men-only camp run by the Italian Red Cross was wedged underneath an overpass and surrounded by fences. Women and children were housed in a church in the city.

The Facebook posts in the months following the eviction documented these developments, often translated into many languages. There were regular hourly updates on the deportations from Ventimiglia to expulsion/detention centres in Southern Italy, or other acts of repression:

> Welcome to Ventimiglia. The rail station is surrounded by police. First bus for deportation left. 25 people [were on the bus]. They confiscated all their mobile phones. (30 May 2016)

> The police entered the church where people without documents seek refuge and has taken all the European activists to identify them. 15 people are detained in the police station in Ventimiglia. The church is guarded by two police vans [text also published in English]. (30 May 2016)

Other posts simultaneously provided political analyses and encouraged people to act:

> After the eviction of camp at the Roya river, a group of migrants built some shelters under a bridge. An awful place, on the riverside of the city but further upstream. [...] The concern is as much about the closure of the border, as about the violence of Italian and French police. The desire to become visible is strong, to reassess their own presence and common will to cross the border. The watchword remains the same: freedom! hurray!' [original text in English, revised]. (16 May 2016)

By sharing these sorts of eyewitness accounts, these Facebook posts provided coverage of an event which did not receive mainstream media attention and also provided alternative perspectives (such as for example about the role of the police). Another example was 'Direct action against *Poste Italiane* [the Italian Mail Service]' Facebook page, which accused the postal service of being actively involved in deporting migrants from Ventimiglia to Southern Italy, by providing the aeroplanes through its company Mistral Air.

Challenging the media construction of the refugee crisis

In addition to the practical organisation of actions, the groups created alternative narratives about the 'refugee crisis'. This included testimonials of both volunteers and migrants – which are not often heard – and alternative analyses. For example, Loredana's post on the BE Facebook page, which told the story of Bashir (a Sudanese asylum seeker), contained peculiar answers to questions like 'Why did you leave your country? Why did you risk the life to come to Europe?

> 'I'm fleeing. From what? Hunger? War? Sister, I'm too tired to explain it to you right now. If you'll be here tomorrow in the morning, I will tell you. Otherwise, do a Google search. I am not fleeing on a whim'. He talks rapidly, in such good English, that I can hardly follow him. [...] 'Sister, I'm here because of a dream. I'm ready to fight, here, to reach France and if I succeed, and I should have children, I will give them a better education. Because it's through education that democratic awareness grows. My generation has no hope. But my child may come back, one day, to my country, which I'm already missing, and teach others how democracy works. The one you have here.' (22 May 2016)

Loredana's comments on Bashir's quote reveal a poignant awareness of the mismatch between Bashir's idealism about European democracy and its failures and impasses: 'I greatly fear we will be disappointed' (22 May 2016).

Another one of Loredana's posts quoting a refugee called 'M' demonstrates a clear awareness of the worlding of conflicts by Western news media:

> 'You forgot about us.' M. speaks a perfect English, he's very handsome, very smart and elegant in his gestures, self-confident but also shy sometimes. He smiles at me. He wants to talk. He is fleeing from Darfur. My memories of the country date back to 2003, as media and the international community stopped to talk about it. He tells me they are not going well at all, supporting his statements with very clever details. Such an expert in geopolitics. '15 years ago, a genocide was taking place. I was happy in the refugee camps, though, because they helped us. NGOs were there. UN agencies were there. We felt supported. I met there two US volunteers, from which I learned my first English. [...] Then, it happened that you stopped talking about us. Now there is Syria. And all the rest. But we continue to kill each other, Arabs and Africans.'(2 September 2016)

These observations about how easily certain countries – particularly those in the Global South – recede from the media spotlight and are forgotten reflects an implicit critique of the Eurocentric nature of media coverage of global conflicts. Even if these comments do not explicitly challenge the media construction or conceptualisation of the news as reflecting global hierarchies of countries and people, they nevertheless show that the agendas of Western media do not go unnoticed among the people caught up in global conflicts, who suffer under these sudden shifts in public attention.

Many of the posts on the NOB Facebook page were written in the style of press releases (potentially seeking coverage from journalists). Commentary accompanied images and videos produced directly by activists themselves, or reposted videos from mainstream media sources, which were consequently reframed from an alternative point of view. For example, one post commented on a video of the *Corriere della Sera*, one of the most popular Italian newspapers:

> Resistance on the rocks continues. The whole area has been militarised. Our settlement has been devastated and plundered. People

> trying to reach the sit-in to give solidarity have been brought to the Police station. Everyone has been threatened with being identified and reported. (30 September 2015)

Prior to the eviction, many posts shared and briefly commented on articles from alternative media sources (*Onda d'urto*, *Ondarossa.info*, *Dinamo Press*, *Internazionale*, *Lettera43*, *Street Politics – Média libre et indépendant*) as well as mainstream news media (*Il Fatto Quotidiano*, *La Repubblica*, *Corriere della Sera*, *La7*) in order to document the activities and encourage participation. Other posts shared Facebook events in other Italian towns organised in solidarity with the struggles in Ventimiglia. For example: 'Police is keeping block border's area [police are continuing to block the border], we are doing breakfast on the rocks. We are not going back' [text published in English] (30 September 2015).

The Facebook page also published testimonies of the migrants themselves, such as a post (13 September 2015) containing excerpts from a letter wrote by a migrant named Fouad in the days spent in prison after the protests at the border. This post expresses a critique of dominant narratives of the 'refugee crisis', focusing on the political dimension of what was going on at the border:

> We broke frontiers! They [police] wanted you to remain alone, *chebabs* [teenage boys in Arabic slang]. They wanted you [activists against borders], boys and girls, to cooperate in silence. They did not succeed, and they never will. They would like to see me going back at the border, afraid of moving on. This is why they hold me in prison. (Fouad, 13 September 2015)

Fouad's analysis of the situation challenges dominant perceptions of the neutrality of the police and the system for processing asylum claims. He also discusses how asylum seekers are isolated by the system and how solidarity from European citizens is actively discouraged. Events and struggles at the border provide the opportunity to contest mainstream media narratives on the 'refugee crisis', as in the following post:

> Today's events reinforce a war against 'migrants' [...]. They contradict [...] media and political narrative that wants to depoliticise 'migrants' condition into a humanitarian crisis and hide the fact that Europe never militarised its borders, and never violently repressed migration flows. (8 September 2015, text published in English)

Here Fouad is situating Europe within the wider geopolitical context – an analysis which is often missing from mainstream news accounts. Other posts contested the credibility of mainstream media coverage of the camp (ANSA and others, especially local newspapers), expressing clear mistrust of institutional politics. Posters clearly felt the No Border movement was the target of a media campaign of denigration and criminalisation, with the migrants depicted as passive subjects:

> Despite the climate of tension fuelled by entrepreneurs of fear, largely widespread in institutional politics, there is plenty of solidarity which arrives here, from Italy and France alike. Stop keeping victimising [us] and treating people as children and passive subjects. There is no one on the camp who is 'managing' someone else: we are all human beings able to react to the situation. People without documents react, in order to take their dignity back, trying to resist a precarious situation and to be free; people acting in solidarity with them react by deciding on which side to stay and providing help in different ways. (22 May 2016)

In September 2016, many posts on the Facebook page not only focused on events in Ventimiglia, but also covered developments in other frontier zones, such as Chiasso at the Italian-Swiss border, where borders have been heavily enforced and people have been stranded. Other posts examined the new agreement between Italian and Sudanese governments about the 'readmission of irregular migrants' (asylum seekers whose claims had been refused[3]). The Facebook page was therefore used as an alternative news source, becoming a national point of reference for all those contesting the mainstream narrative and institutional border-control approach to migration.

Anti-immigrant groups on Facebook: conspiratorial responses to dysfunction and distrust

This chapter so far has focused on the responses of migrants and sympathetic European citizens to the dysfunction and breakdown of trust in the governance and media coverage. As discussed, these focused primarily on practical support and in some cases providing alternative narratives in the face of hostile media coverage. More radical perspectives also challenged some of the dominant humanitarian narratives which presume the neutrality of borders and border police, thereby ignoring the contradictions between demands for integration and the isolation resulting from the conditions of the asylum system. The following pages will explore the responses of those who are hostile to immigration, and how they interpreted the systemic failures and breakdown of trust. As will be seen, for those hostile to immigration, official responses to the 'refugee crisis' were interpreted as emblematic of ungovernability and state breakdown fuelling conspiracy theories about demographic change, miscegenation and the spread of Islam. These are strongly inflected by ethnonationalist conceptions of identity in which European citizenship is seen to be synonymous with whiteness, as well as highly gendered conceptions of the migrant, the citizen and the role of the state.

We studied one Facebook group in the UK and one in Italy with strong anti-immigration, anti-refugee, anti-Islam views. Unlike the pro-migrant groups, which were mostly dedicated to practical activities, these last two groups were mostly online platforms for sharing articles from Breitbart and other right-wing blogs, as well as the re-posting and reframing of news according to a right-wing perspective. There has been significant scholarship on the use of the internet and social media platforms by the far-right (see for example Daniels 2009, 2013; Ekman 2014, 2018; Neumayer 2016). Facebook is considered to be a site for the like-minded, and 'provides at least the impression of a particular intimacy' (Neumayer 2016), For this reason, it can be a site for racist and xenophobic 'counter-publics' (Neumayer 2016). As Johan Farkas, Jannick Schou and Christine Neumayer observe, the socio-technical structure of Facebook can 'shape new modalities of antagonism', which they term 'platformed antagonism' (Farkas, Schou and Neumayer 2018, 464). They argue that:

> These discursive practices not only relied on the production of text, but also on the social media platform's facilitation of concealed personal identities, construction of fake accounts and algorithmic dissemination of aggressive posts, images and videos. As sites of platformed antagonism, the interactive characteristics of Facebook became a means of struggle and hostility between two ethno-cultural identities, constructed as fundamentally incompatible by both the Facebook pages and a majority of commenting users. (Farkas, Schou and Neumayer 2018, 475)

The Facebook groups we studied included:

- Refugees Not Welcome (RNW), a UK-based right populist anti-refugee Facebook page with 3,106 likes and 3,100 followers (as of 5 November 2018).
- Stop Invasione (SI) an Italy-based anti-immigrant Facebook page, with 18,466 people likes and 19,002 followers (as of 9 August 2018). During 2019 the page changed its name to 'Contro l'invasione pacifica' (against peaceful invasion). The number of likes dropped to 10.936, with 10.973 followers.

Members of these groups held a general consensus around refugees not really needing protection and entering Western countries just to take advantage of generous welfare provisions, or for terrorism, crime and other sinister purposes. Unlike the solidarity Facebook groups mentioned earlier, RNW and SI did not focus on practical action, alternative news and narratives. Instead, they primarily involved sharing and commenting on national and international news. SI sourced at least half their news from mainstream outlets – notably from across the political spectrum – re-framing these articles through commenting or manipulating the content to fit sensationalist anti-immigration reporting. An anti-immigrant blog called *Italiani pacifici contro il buonismo* (pacific Italians against do-goodery), was also used, as well as far-right websites (*Riscatto Nazionale*; *Primato Nazionale*). Although RNW is an English-language, UK account, the news stories were global. *The Local* was a common source (an English-language expat news source in various countries), along with *Breitbart* and *Russia Today*.

The posts and stories which were shared repeatedly demonstrated the same argument: Black and Asian people, especially Muslim men, should not be let into the UK, Italy or other Western countries. This argument creates a chain of equivalence between refugees, immigrants, racialised European citizens, Muslims and terrorists. It is based on a construction of these categories of people as essentially aggressive, violent, barbaric, hyper-masculine sexual predators, rapists, thieves and religious extremists. This enables feelings of hate and fear to be projected onto racialised bodies. The intention of posts seemed to be about provoking moral outrage rather than action. The distrust in the mainstream media, national governments and EU institutions articulated in these Facebook groups was not based in a critical perspective, making it very different from the scepticism of media coverage of conflicts discussed earlier. Instead, it was rooted in anxieties about the loss of Western dominance, as well as concerns about the lack of economic resources for facing mass arrivals of migrants, thus contributing to an ethnic competition with 'indigenous people' and a demographic threat (Ekman 2018). Wealthy, European nations were presented as innocent victims, erasing legacies of colonial violence and oppression. National identities were perceived as essences (Huntington 2004 cited in Muthyala 2006) with which Islam is seen to be fundamentally incompatible, hence the extreme scepticism towards the possibility of integration.

Conspiratorial framings

Some of the articles posted on the RNW's and SI's pages were fake news, but conspiracy news or conspiratorial framings of news were actually more common. This included far-right blogs with neutral, bland web design (presumably to give them the credibility of mainstream news) but with inflammatory and conspiratorial content. The organisations promoted by the Facebook pages took a similar approach by presenting themselves in neutral terms. For example, the Gatestone Institute (which featured on the SI Facebook page in relation to reports about migrant rapists), defined itself as 'a non-partisan, not-for-profit international policy council and think tank', 'dedicated to educating the public about what the mainstream media fails to report' (Gatestone Institute 2018). Formerly called Stonegate Institute and Hudson New York, the Gatestone Institute is in reality a right-wing, anti-Muslim US-based think tank, which has attracted attention several times for publishing false articles and being a source of viral falsehoods. For instance, the fact-checking website Snopes has found multiple false viral stories originating with Gatestone. One such was example involved claims that in London – called 'Londonistan' in the piece – 423 mosques were built 'on the sad ruins of English Christianity', as 500 churches closed. However, the story cherry-picked the data to ignore hundreds of newly opened churches (Fang 2018).

In other cases, the stories themselves were not actually fake, but posters framed them in conspiratorial terms through selectively quoting information. For example, one article was shared on RNW's page about a shooting at a cinema in Germany, in which the police were quoted as saying that they did not suspect terrorist motives, while an 'anonymous source' claimed that the act was carried out by Islamic extremists and that the suspect spoke in 'broken German' (24 June 2016). The poster drew attention to the anonymous source and did not mention the police testimonial at all. Another post (29 October 2016), on SI's page, contained a reference to the role of

NGOs which are active in search and rescue operations in the Mediterranean, depicted as being part of a business ('the immigration business'), in secret co-operation with human traffickers to deposit all immigrants in Italy.

Whilst the pro-migrant groups used voluntary acts of kindness, goodwill or active solidarity in the struggle for freedom of movement to counter official anti-immigrant hostility, the conspiratorial framings used by RNW and SI were more consistent with right-wing populism: they represented real, genuine people as opposed to immigrants, their allies and powerful players of 'the system' (finance, foreign powers), etc. They saw their enemies as actively encouraging immigration to populate Europe with Africans and Muslims, thereby making white European Christians a minority. The governments of the UK, Italy and other Western countries were seen to be taken liberal dupes; mainstream media were accused of feeding a sanctimonious 'do-gooder attitude'; and white Europeans were generally perceived as vulnerable and gullible because of their sympathy to immigrants or hidden sense of guilt, and at worst as race traitors. European generosity, democratic tolerance and support infrastructure to help those in need were seen to be taken advantage of by amoral, deceitful, ungrateful migrants. This is generally consistent with the 'producerist' ideology intrinsic to populism, as Jan Werner Müller argues:

> Populists pit the pure, innocent, always hardworking people against a corrupt elite who do not really work (other than to further their self-interest), and, in right wing populism, also against the very bottom of society (those who do not really work and live like parasites off the work of others). (Müller 2016: 23)

This resentment towards those at the bottom of society – and in particular refugees – was quite evident. For example, the most popular post in the sample of RNW's page featured a news story posted on 26 June 2016 about migrants breaking into a clothing donations bin in Germany. The post received multiple likes and comments, including 'put them down' and comparisons with monkeys, characteristic of the 'animalisation' marking right-wing discourses on migrants (Vaughan-Williams 2015). The poster framed this in terms of migrants taking away clothes that were needed by vulnerable and elderly Europeans. The poster presented migrants as breaking into the bin because of being 'unsatisfied with the clothing provided by the government, so they search for more expensive, usually brand name clothing' (26 June 2016). The post included the sharing of a video clip which was directly uploaded to Facebook, with no mention of the source. Despite this being impossible to verify as news, the raw, hand-held quality of the footage lent it a particular immediacy and authenticity; the conspiratorial framing suggested it could reveal the ugly truth that the liberal mainstream media wanted to hide. Visual innuendo was also used to create conspiratorial narratives. For example, one of the posts on RNW included an internet meme showing an image of Ahmed Mohammed (the boy in the US who brought a digital clock to school which was mistaken for a bomb) with a caption reading 'don't forget to set your bombs back' (30 October 2016). The meme was a response to media outcry about Ahmed Mohammed's mistreatment, and implied that he really was trying to make a bomb. It functions as a kind of in-joke, drawing the audience together – those who really 'know the truth'.

In the case of SI's page, the main conspirational framing was so-called 'white genocide' or 'ethnic substitutionism': the idea that obscure global powers are conspiring to substitute the white population with Black people. One of the quoted references to such plans (31 May 2016) was a report issued by the United Nations in 2000 entitled 'Replacement Migration: Is it a Solution to Declining and Ageing Populations?' In the report, 'replacement migration' refers to the level of migration which would be necessary in order to prevent population decline resulting from an ageing population and declining birth rates. Such demographic arguments (which present immigration as a solution for the problems of ageing populations in the West) open the ground for right-wing moral panics around 'substitution'. Another post (14 October 2016) made similar arguments about ethnic substitution "Western governments are letting [immigration] destroy our society and do not allow the people to defend themselves. Is populism the problem? No, it's the invasion!" A picture below the text juxtaposed two images: Black people with open arms asking for help in a boat (under the title 'Import') and beautiful young white people who had just received their degrees (under the title 'Export'). The reference here is to the fact that Italy has a problem of emigration among young, university-educated people. The interpretation of this phenomenon is that Italy suffers from the loss of skilled professionals, who are then replaced with unskilled Africans (Africans are assumed to be unskilled).

Conclusion

We have discussed how migrants, their supporters and those opposed to immigration have responded to the institutional failures of migration governance as it breaks down while trying to meet both humanitarian and securitarian demands. The asylum system is the cruellest expression of this, as people must use dangerous and clandestine means to reach Europe, face hardship and destitution once they get there, and are faced with labyrinthine bureaucracy. For migrants and their supporters, this meant setting up ad-hoc mutual aid systems to share information and practical solidarity, facilitated by mobile media and social media platforms. For those forced to use clandestine means to travel, the sharing economy was used as a measure for determining trust and credibility. Offering alternative messages was also important, whether this meant the production of alternative news (as in the two Italian examples) or simply the sharing of positive messages in order to boost morale in the face of increasingly dominant anti-immigrant attitudes. Social media platforms such as WhatsApp and Facebook often became useful in co-ordinating this support; in the absence of state support or legal means to reach Europe, indicators of the sharing economy (such as the number of Facebook friends) became the only measure of trustworthiness. There is not enough to discuss this fully, but it is important to consider the wider implications of a situation where platforms owned by unaccountable Silicon Valley tech giants become the only means to organise this support when institutions fail, and people fall through the cracks.

For those opposed to immigration, the dysfunction of migration governance fuelled conspiracy theories, particularly about white genocide, the existence of a shadowy global elite who want to import a cheap labour force to undercut local wages, and the incompatibility of Islam with liberal democracies. The social/technical features of social media were used to promote such 'platformed antagonism' (Farkas, Schou and Neumayer 2018). Various techniques were used to give these conspiracies credibility, including the reframing or selective quoting of mainstream news stories to give them a conspiratorial angle, or the reference to right-wing conspiracy blogs which had a clean and neutral web design to make them appear like official organisations.

The Facebook pages in Italy supported more militant action than in the UK, possibly reflecting different activist traditions, histories of alternative spaces and the different ways such campaigns relate to liberal humanitarian politics or radical Left traditions (for example No Borders campaigns). The anti-immigration sentiment in Italy seemed to also be much stronger – and this needs to be understood in relation to the public attitudes which ultimately brought the anti-immigrant right coalition government to power. Disturbingly, the attitudes held by the anti-immigrant groups seem to now be accepted as common sense across the political spectrum. Hopefully, we have offered some insights about how such views take on credibility.

Notes

1 The Gukurahundi was a series of massacres carried out in Zimbabwe on the Nebdele people from 1983 to 1987 by the Zimbabwe National Army.

2 'Ode to Joy' was sung by residents of Munich on the arrival of the refugees. For a clip from BBC News showing this, see https://www.bbc.com/news/av/world-europe-34162844/migrant-crisis-applause-as-hundreds-arrive-in-munich. Accessed 25 September 2018.

3 See *Memorandum of Understanding between the Italian and the Sudanese Ministry of Interiors for Fighting Criminality, Managing Borders and Immigration Flows, and in the Matter of Repatriation*, signed on 3 August 2016: Link to the memorandum: https://www.meltingpot.org/IMG/pdf/accordo-polizia-italia-sudan_rev.pdf. Accessed 20 August 2018.

Interlude 3

How it feels to be made a migrant: restrictions, frustration and longing

This interlude is based on the discussions in which participants in Birmingham discussed how it felt to be made a migrant, and the constraints and frustrations they continually faced. Inspired by Frigaa Haug's memory work, we took participants through a workshop process where we shared anonymised quotes, songs and video clips generated so far through the interview process with small groups of three to four people. We used this material to spark discussions about shared experiences so that these stories would not be interpreted as isolated individual anecdotes, but would instead draw out broader structural conditions and wider global inequalities. This process foregrounds the imaginative aspects of memory (Keightley and Pickering 2012) in which individuals reframe and map their experiences in relation to others. As part of the group discussions, we took the individuals through visualisation exercises and asked them to think of images and metaphors which they felt captured the discussion. Based on the visualisations, we created photomontages. The images reflect the participants' experience of continual constraint, rejection and shunning by British society, as well as double standards and inequality.[1]

The first image is of a woman who is a relationship with a man who does not love her any more (see Figure 1). They have had children together and they still live together, but she is reminded every day of how the love has gone. However, she still hopes the love will come back someday. This image came out of the discussion

Figure 1: Visualisation: being in a marriage when the man doesn't want you anymore, 2017.

about the experience of the asylum process (the continual waiting for an immigration decision being similar to the agonisations of unrequited love), as well as the frustrations of being perceived as always being an outsider. It is implied in the description that the woman is trapped in the relationship and that she and her children are possibly financially dependent on the husband and cannot leave, which speaks to the dependencies and constraints of the immigration system.

Figure 2: Visualisation: man with luggage who can't go inside his house, 2017.

The second image (Figure 2) also speaks to the condition of being a continual outsider; it is marked by similar feelings of longing and frustration. A man stands outside his house with his luggage; he is at the gate and the door is open, but he is not allowed to go inside. It emerged out of discussions about what it meant to be treated as a migrant, in which quotes were shared about how other participants had defined this. Participants spoke of feelings of floating, being neither here nor there, and being an outcast:

> R1: I think for me that when you're called a migrant, you feel like you are trespassing [...]. You are here but you are not wanted because you don't have the proper status. So you are floating somewhere. Because also you can't go back to your country.
>
> R2: You don't belong here. That's why you are a migrant. That's the feeling I'm having. Outcast. Abandoned. Left out. An outsider. (Group discussion, 22 May 2017)

The third image (Figure 3) is of someone who is looking at custard or an appetising-looking cake but is unable to buy and eat it because

Figure 3: Visualisation: man looking at sweets who is unable to buy them because he only gets £37.50/week, 2017.

he only has £37.50 (the amount allocated to asylum seekers who are awaiting a decision), which only allows for purchasing the barest necessities. He is hungry and craves these treats but can only look at them. Like the other images, it speaks to the constraints of life under the asylum system, and the longing for the full life that seems tantalisingly close but which has been denied – as one of the participants says, 'you are in a prison but not in a prison' (Group discussion, 22 May 2017).

The fourth image (Figure 4) is of someone who is frightened; the police are watching but not doing anything to help. It was in response to a discussion of one of the interview quotes where the interviewee tells a story (discussed in detail in the following chapter) about his rubbish bins being vandalised the day after the Brexit vote, and the police told him that nothing could be done; he saw this lack of action as a exemplifying institutionalised racism in the

Figure 4: Visualisation: policeman who does nothing to help frightened people, 2017.

police force, which leads Black people to be treated with suspicion – as potential criminals – but never taken seriously as victims of crime. The participants also spoke of similar experiences:

> R1: I was in a situation in London, around that time. I took a man to the police because he had broken into the house and taken all my belongings. When we went to the police, they just said, there's nothing we can do. Go back home. So we cannot trust the police. But if it was a Black man, they would have …
>
> R2: They would have gone through the cameras to check. (Group discussion, 22 May 2017)

The fifth image (Figure 5) was of a white, British man telling a group of African and Asian immigrants that they are ignorant fools who are wicked and evil. It is in response to discussions about

You can draw a group of people sitting down and one person standing up and telling them,
"you are fools" "You are wicked, you are evil"

.Who will be the one standing? And who will be the people telling others that they are fools?
R1: They are white, they are British, telling people
sit down, immigrants….So if you have a big old British man with a big stomach, telling all these people that we are fools.

Figure 5: Visualisation: man telling people they are evil and they are fools, 2017.

the presence of Europeans in their countries, and how colonialism was internalised by those there (as one participant says, 'they taught us to be beggars'):

> R1: This is how they changed our country for us, to feel, to feel belittled. Because the plan was that they replace the old, ancient education system, which they managed to do, and they changed our culture.

> R2: You see, they taught us to be beggars. There was no-one begging at that time. No-one asking for everything. But now, look at how many are beggars out there who are from our countries.

Figure 6: 'Life in Handcuffs', 2017 by Prabjot Kaur. Oil on canvas.

The sense of constraint was most profoundly expressed through a painting created by Prabjot Kaur, an artist and one of the participants in the Nottingham workshops. Titled 'Life in Handcuffs', it is a self-portrait of a woman in handcuffs (Figure 6). It is based on her own experiences and was also inspired by a group discussion in which people shared experiences of how the immigration system made them feel trapped and how they were unable to work, study or otherwise live a normal life. This also served as the basis of a newspaper spoof and a scene in the theatrical performance (discussed in the following chapter and interlude). The image of constraint in the painting is not about the restrictions on freedom that one might conventionally expect of conflict zones outside the West; it is not the sad story of flight, so much as the impossible conditions of life in the UK.

Notes

1 The images can be seen at http://conflictmemorydisplacement.com/online-exhibition/. Accessed 30 September 2019.

4

The processes of migrantification: how displaced people are made into 'migrants'

Introduction

This chapter reflects on the insights of feminist practices of memory work and what such an approach can bring to analyses of being constituted as 'migrant' in the UK and Italy, based on the interviews and workshops we carried out in both countries. The chapter argues that no one is born a migrant: people are constructed as 'migrants' through the manner in which they are positioned and treated by public institutions, the media and other members of society. These processes construct the identity of 'migrant' as the pre-eminent aspect of any individual, flattening out other aspects of their personality and experience. More generally, in a world where directions and players of global politics appear to have become less certain or knowable, the manner in which people are made to be 'migrants' reveals some important lessons about bordering and the exercise of sovereignty in our time.

The chapter argues that this institutionalised 'becoming migrant' has parallels with processes of gendering as it has been deconstructed by critical memory work and, similarly, demands a critical denaturalising. We use this work to argue for critical attention to be given to to the process of 'migrantification' that is extending to many locations, becoming among the most naturalised and commonsensical attributions of human worth and entitlement, with the most deadly of consequences for those who fail. Our account builds on the extensive and insightful work outlining practices of bordering as practices of ordering and disciplining the spaces of civil society (Yuval-Davis, Wemyss and Cassidy 2017; 2019). From this work we understand that the border has extended and become dispersed across space and across practices. As a result, the encounter with the border ceases to be a discrete *assessment* of status and becomes an endless demand to *demonstrate* status.

The process of 'migrantification' runs alongside these practices of everyday bordering. Some aspects of being made a 'migrant' arise from the formal attributions of status administered through the state, including the extensive network of policing practices that makes up 'bordering'. Yet 'migrantification' is always more than these formal practices alone. It includes the popular take-up of bordering logics and the infiltration of such logics into any and every human encounter. It occurs also through the drip-feed of popular media, reminding all of their position in a hierarchy of insiders, outsiders and those waiting for decisions. Perhaps the sense of loss of all human exiles throughout history floats in and out of these located experiences of being made 'migrant', and perhaps also the processes of 'migrantification' seek to colonise this other migrant consciousness, mobilising the most personal and formative of experiences as a mode of encouraging the internalisation of this other constructed and instrumental categorisation as 'migrant'.

Learning from memory work – how to denaturalise social identities

It is this colonising of personal experience while also inserting people into highly structured and constraining categories of being that echoes analyses of processes of gendering. In particular, we looked back to ways of thinking about becoming 'woman' that excavated gendering as something akin to a life-long process of brain-washing, violent when required, always insistent, promising to give meaning to the most personal and the most disruptive of life experiences. Unlike analyses that privilege reminiscence as a route to rebuilding life narratives, we borrowed the very different conception of memory work pioneered by Frigga Haug. This is an approach to critical analyses of memories in a collective forum for the purposes of uncovering and dismantling dominant processes of gendering. It is a way of working that arose from an earlier phase in the women's movement and retains the democratising impulse of its formation. Haug, famously, developed approaches to collective analysis of social processes, bringing together the shared memories and analysis of groups of women. She has described this process as a collapsing of the binary of subject and object, instead uncovering participants in such collective projects as 'experts on everyday life'. She explains this project:

> Since this everyday life is where society reproduces itself, an understanding of it would … modify each individual's attitude towards herself and to others. One would take oneself and others seriously. Questions about how social structures … are perceived, modified and endured by me in my everyday life, and how others deal with the same structures, would transform us all, without our fully realising it, into experts on our everyday life. (Haug 1992: 19)

As part of this critical approach to social identities, Haug asked also whether those who had passed through the processes of becoming 'woman' should be regarded as 'victims' or 'culprits'. With the benefit of our additional decades of shared study, we might consider this (partly tongue-in-cheek) distinction to be misleading – and instead consider the overlapping processes of internalisation, identification, coercion and social pressure that combine to create 'feminine' subjects, with an awareness of the central role of self-making in these practices. At one level, this account of the victim/culprit seems to have no connection to the experience of those made 'migrants'. However, as we will go on to discuss, the processes of making people into 'migrants' may run alongside the deeply emotional experiences of displacement, exile and nostalgia. Although structured as among the most abstract and dehumanising of constructs, the making of the 'migrant' also incorporates some aspects of personal narratives and experiences, including tactics developed to cope with a hostile environment.

In our interviews held in London, Birmingham and Nottingham in the UK, and in Pisa and Bologna in Italy, we asked people who had been displaced by conflict to reflect critically on how they have been constructed as migrants in their encounters with the state, public institutions, media and other members of society. We then held workshops with the interviewees, inspired by Haug's critical memory work, where we shared anonymised quotes from other interviewees. We asked them to react to these quotes, and to think collectively of general notions, metaphors and images that could express the general meaning of their experiences of 'migrantification'.

What we have sought to take from Haug is a framework that can both give space to experience a well as multiple interpretations and reflections on experience, and also offer a language to unpack the manner in which categories enforced through threat and violence can come to be regarded as natural, spontaneous and permanent. In our conversations it became apparent that the attribution of the label 'migrant' was accepted, in part, because life events appeared to coincide with this attribution, but also, in part, because inhabiting this attribution was demanded in so many interchanges with others.

None of this is to deny that the taking of identity names comes fraught with difficulties. We all understood that we have learned to identify the 'migrant' in a context of extreme politicisation of population movements and a rapidly changing language of classification and demarcation. In part this is in response to the intensive vilification of migrants, in the press and in political language. Whereas previous eras might have identified 'foreigners' or 'outsiders', the active construction of the category 'migrant' is a more recent endeavour. As a result, we can see that the status of migrant may coincide with a positioning outside national belonging, but it is the residue of movement – the fact of being trapped into this status no matter what personal or familiar histories one may have – that marks this category. In an attempt to make visible what is happening in this process of marking/categorising/excluding, we sought to chart the processes of 'migrantification', taking the critical standpoint of those who passed through them.

Why 'migrantification'?

Our ability to recognise processes that naturalise particular identities has been enhanced by jarring neologisms, with the unexpected and/or ugly conglomeration of partly familiar and partly new combinations of sounds shaking up comprehension. Notable in the field of migration studies are the coinages of 'crimmigration' as a frame to understand the collapsing together of immigration and criminal legislative processes (Stumpf 2006) and 'hostipitality' to indicate the transformation of structures of reception into expressions of hostility (McFadyen 2016). Similarly, we propose the portmanteau of 'migrantification' to redirect attention to the active practices that position people as 'migrants' and work to solidify this status as an ongoing category of identity.

So we offer this neologism in full knowledge that it is forced and uncomfortable to say, in the hope that the twist of this verbal discomfort can make apparent the contortions that go into the making of 'migrants'. We must reiterate again that this making into 'migrants' is not a matter that springs fully formed from the phenomenon of population movement. We have known others to move in not so distant times (and perhaps in other places) and these others did not occupy the role of 'migrant' as it has been constructed more recently. Even today, we see that not all of those in movement become 'migrants' – some become 'ex-pats', others 'bogus', others still 'victims' of trafficking, of warlords, of natural disaster, of ethnic hatred, of economic collapse.

Migrantification offers a term to sew together the varying techniques that position people in movement in one or other of these sub-categories while still highlighting the over-arching process of making people into 'migrants' in contexts where 'migrant' signals a social and political identity and a formal status in the eyes of the state. Migrantification seeks to describe both of these strands – the state-defined legal status and the looser but still suffocating imposition of 'migrantness' by others. In fact, it is this odd mutuality between the practices of the state and the interchanges of civil society that marks out 'migrantification'.

Recent years of vociferous anti-migrant campaigns coupled with increasingly brutal practices undertaken in the name of border control have solidified the category of 'migrant'. There have been attempts to diversify the language used to describe the movement of people, to assist in categorisation and to differentiate between varieties of need and entitlement. Such attempts can be discerned both in the invention of the 'asylum seeker' (Fekete 2001; Goodman and Speer 2007) and in the diligent activity of polling companies in mapping popular attitudes to migrants of differing kinds (Blinder and Richards 2018).

The majority of the people who helped us to understand the process of being made a 'migrant' were or had been in the asylum process. Some had achieved refugee status and some in Britain had taken British citizenship (this was not the case in Italy). Others had had asylum claims refused and were living through the painful uncertainty of appeals. Much of what we have gathered arises from the fraught processes of displacement. However, we have continued to use the general term of 'migrant' to shape our questions and discussion.

Our view is that the construction is of a generic, paradigmatic Other – a perpetual foreigner, a being continually marked by a history of mobility – and is a phenomenon of our moment of hyper-politicisation of population movements across proliferating and increasingly militarised borders. Although many 'migrants' have far luckier and far more affluent and secure lives than many of our project participants, we did not wish to distinguish between the insights of 'asylum seekers', 'refugees' and 'citizens'. Instead the process of being displaced by conflict and then remaking a life elsewhere, in the midst of the most hostile of environments, linked the commentary of all and suggested a route to understanding what happens to make the status of 'migrant' appear so conspicuous and so inescapable. Inevitably, given the migrant-baiting/hating climate across Europe and beyond, significant proportions of this discussion focused on techniques of containment, 'differential inclusion' (Mezzadra and Neilson 2013), hierarchisation and dehumanisation. However, we tried to avoid replaying this well-known and highly painful narrative, not least because these processes are well documented already. Instead, we tried to find ways to make visible the small day-to-day occurrences that created or confirmed the status of 'migrant'.

We phrased our questions around the experience of being made into a 'migrant', stressing our interest in the practices that create and confirm this status within British and Italian society. Understandably, some participants highlighted the differentiation of different bodies in movement through differential entitlement:

> Well, personally, I think there's a difference between, like, an immigrant and an asylum seeker. As an immigrant, you know, you are a second-class citizen, but you're allowed to do, you know, basic things like work, go to school, go on holiday. Simple things, you know, like any human being should be able to do. At the moment I don't think I'm immigrant, I'm not a migrant. I'm just nobody, you know, like, I don't have the right to anything, you know. That's how I feel about that. (Birmingham, 3 March 2017)

However, despite the detailed accounts of the particular dehumanising bureaucracy of the asylum process, others recognised the existence of a 'migrantness' that went beyond formal status and, it seemed, might be passed down through generations. In particular, people spoke of their own children who were born in Britain and also of the status of members of the research team who were racially minoritised, and therefore forever marked as 'migrant'. The genealogy of the person seeking asylum or the 'migrant' was seen to expand from being a question of status to include questions of lineage:

> R1: When you try and tell British people that they are British born, they are not English, people still look at them as immigrant people. That stamp, I think it is forever there. I don't think there is anything they can do to erase it. They will always say you just come here to drag things here.
>
> R2: They can equally say this person was born to an asylum parent that came to seek asylum, they will say it in that manner. (Nottingham, 19 April 2017)

Much of the description of state actions to create 'migrants' returned to the labyrinthine processes of the asylum system. This, of course, was the context through which the majority of our participants had encountered the border-making state. Moreover, within the 'European migration crisis' (bogus) asylum seekers implicitly became the popular paradigm of the migrants: a kind of 'refugeesation' of the imaginary concerning non-national, non-European populations took place. However, even within this asylum-centred analysis, connections were made to other formal 'categories' of migrant. The process of being made into a 'migrant' was understood as both the state bureaucracies and of public service providers, and as the more diffuse feeling of unease that spread across life in Britain and Italy.

In order to understand this configuration of state bureaucracy in the service of dehumanisation and racisms that are remade to identify 'migrantness' as a category, we might consider modes of migrantification as an agglomeration not a sequence. Much of what is described here arises from the machinery surrounding the claiming of asylum. We chose to speak to those displaced by conflict and, therefore, the majority of our participants had encountered the demands of the asylum claim whatever route they had taken into Europe. We have continued to use the catch-all of 'migrant' here because it avoids the further categorisations of the asylum and immigration process, as well as the moralising distinctions between the refugee and the 'economic migrant'. Instead of seeking to differentiate between the experiences of those in differing stages or with differing outcomes in the process of seeking to regularise status, we continue to use the term 'migrantification' as a way of mapping the assembly of techniques in play. To extend the borrowing from Haug, in the mapping of female sexualisation it is possible to identify the overlaps and continuities between the becoming woman of good and bad girls, of housewives and of emancipated women, of all women regardless of their particular niche status within the terms of womanhood. Similarly, seeking to identify the process of migrantification as it makes a range of people into migrants, not only into more precise legal statuses, can help us to understand the logic that forms a backdrop to the more legalistic determinations of identity and belonging.

When you realise that you are 'a migrant'

When trying to denaturalise the concept of the 'migrant', we needed to imagine what it was not to think of yourself as a 'migrant'. We were interested in the moment/s of recognition when people understood that others viewed them as 'migrants', the 'aha' moment described in Fanon's experience of hearing a child call 'mummy, mummy, look a black man' and then realising that the 'black man' was him (Fanon 1986). The realisation that you have been taken for a 'migrant' is described in similar terms. People learn to see themselves as 'migrants' when they see through the eyes of others. It is the expression of animosity, of aversion, that signals the categorisation; as one participant says, 'you can feel it, the look on their face, and their tone of voice, yes' (Birmingham, 3 March 2017).

The accounts of realising that you have become this other thing, a 'migrant' – and are destined to occupy this role for the foreseeable (and unforeseeable) future – begin all too often with incidents of aggression, disrespect and what we might once have called 'aversion'. It is to be noted, however, that our participants do not seek to naturalise this racism. Unlike the accounts of aversive racism as an inherent human trait in the face of difference, we were told of the factors that trigger such aversive reactions. The impact of ongoing vilification arose repeatedly in our discussions:

> You know when they hear about asylum seekers, as if, like, they're diseased. We are diseased. We are now like contagious disease. We have the contagious disease. Come on, honestly. Yes. (Birmingham, 10 March 2017)

Whether familiar with Mary Douglas's account of purity and danger (2002) or not, participants explained the day-to-day impact of dehumanising discourses in the media and in wider political life. Alongside the practices of the UK Home Office and the Italian Ministry of Interiors which constrained day-to-day existence, the repeated vilification of asylum seekers and of all migrants in popular media and in the language of mainstream political parties created an amplifying loop of stigmatisation, a kind of rumour-mill that spread suspicion and unease throughout society.

This led to some contradictory analyses. On the one hand, it was agreed by UK participants that the wider population understood little about populations in movement, evidenced by an inability to distinguish between those who had been displaced recently and those born in Britain, albeit to migrant families. On the other, it was clear that some key terms of immigration control had infiltrated everyday life, largely as new forms of stigma. In particular, the status of 'asylum seeker' was regarded as a highly stigmatised identity and, as a result, participants chose not to reveal this 'status' in their day-to-day interactions.

> We don't mention the word asylum. Never ever, you mention, as I said, honestly. You never mention that we are asylum seekers because,

if you did, like, they'd speak to you as a contagious disease. (Birmingham, 10 March 2017)

Like, when they hear those words, they get serious. Like, if they smile, they stop smiling. They stop smiling. (Birmingham, 10 March 2017)

The process of learning to see oneself as a 'migrant' occurred, for our participants, in a context where mobility has become increasingly stigmatised. Many of our participants pointed to media antagonism to migrants as a factor in understanding themselves as holding this status (see Philo, Briant and Donald 2013). Our interviewees explained that they were facing the consequences of a concerted campaign to vilify migrants, undertaken by mainstream political parties and amplified by popular media.

The encouragement of a structure of feeling that positions people in movement as a dangerous contagion was regarded as an effective but unfortunate fear story, something that created and fuelled anxiety for no good reason. It was impressed upon us that this scare-story arose from a concerted demonisation of migrants, although the origin of such suspicion remained unclear.

R1: I think they make it so big, as something that is taboo. Everyone here; we are all migrants, we are all immigrants, so as we move, they move as well. That is life. Life is all about migrants, I know, everybody moves around. They will be like I don't want to stay in the UK again, I want to go to Spain, I want to go with my family down there, so we all move around there. So, we are all migrants.

R2: Even life moves, because it doesn't stay. (Nottingham, 19 April 2017)

At the same time, it was understood that this positioning as 'migrant' arose from the internal political battles of European societies:

So I feel all the time that I am an immigrant because … a big chunk of the politics is about immigration so any party from UKIP to the Conservatives, the Labour Party, anyone wants to play like a game,

> start speaking about immigration … start speaking about immigration then the [poll] lead will go high. (Birmingham, 10 March 2017)

Being defined by others

In an echo of canonical theories of race and racism, we heard that an early component of being made a 'migrant' arose from processes of categorisation from without (Omi and Winant 1994). For some, this involved a necessary tolerance towards the terminology used to name their experience and, through this, their status and identity. More generally, categorisation was identified as a technique of day-to-day hierarchisation and discrimination, with state bureaucracies bleeding violently into everyday life:

> First, there's tourism, second, their dogs, third, Polish people, fourth, homeless people and then we come. Yes, there's a sequence of the British diagram. Okay? We are last. We are last to come. (Birmingham, 10 March 2017)

The practice of categorisation was regarded as an aspect of wider dehumanisation, part of a seemingly never-ending process of being assessed, passed on, placed in line – all as part of a process of application that appeared to be designed to break the spirit of those applying.

> In the UK, they torture, but mentally torture you. I think they use science to help to torture people. It's more painful than any torture, honestly, any torture. … and they give you a long, long process. They don't issue your paperwork in order to torture you to make it further, to make you sick. It would have been very difficult to recover. Honestly, the suffering you have in this country. (Birmingham, 10 March 2017)

Categorisation, therefore, goes beyond a moment of initial label-giving and continues as a never concluded process of appraisal. In processes of migrantification, however, it is unlikely that the categorised can avoid, adapt or refuse their attribution. While processes such as gendering have been radically re-made through the impact of popular feminism and accompanying adaptations and refusals by men, women and those identifying as non-binary, those caught up in the theatre of migrantification remain vulnerable to the exclusions of formal bordering. This intertwining of legal and cultural practices limited the ability of those marked as 'migrants' to refuse their categorisation or to adapt or extend categorising narratives. These constraints were demonstrated to us in the explanation of a young woman who had learned to accept her categorisation as a 'victim of trafficking':

> I would say yes and no, because like she said I've been here twelve years as well, but then when you go to the Home Office or when you seek asylum it's kind of been drummed into your ear. It's just like my case is under trafficking and at first it was like do you know what trafficking is and they explained it to me. And then it kind of had to get to the stage where I had to identify myself as one, so sometimes it got to the process of, every time I want to say, I can't really say it out [loud] so they say I am, so that [is] was they call me. But do I want to be? But then I think I don't want to be called that. They say I am this, they say I am that, but obviously eventually I started saying okay, I am a trafficking victim. (Nottingham, 19 April 2017)

The formal component of migrantification demands acceptance of the categorisation given. Without this acceptance, and more than this, without a re-narration of experience to confirm the correctness of the given category, those seeking to regularise their status risk everything. Their chance to build a safe life and to escape the never-ending insecurity, hardship and disrespect of immigration control rests on a willing and convincing performance of their allocated category.

Another speaker explained how the complexities that placed her outside the established categorisations of immigration law brought further stigma, not least as a result of how little was understood about the complexities of the asylum process in the wider population,

> For me, if I don't know a person I will not go out of my way to say, I am waiting for my whatever … It's my personal private story anyway, so I wouldn't just come out and just say, oh, hello, I'm waiting for my status. It's also difficult to explain my status because I'm not an asylum seeker and I'm not a refugee, so there's no label on me at the moment, except illegal immigrant. I wouldn't go around saying, oh, hi, I'm an illegal immigrant to anybody. (Nottingham, 19 April 2017)

Living under suspicion and control

Being a migrant, for our participants, was about living a strictly circumscribed existence. This living under control included experiences of surveillance, restrictions on personal freedom, restricted spaces for intimacy and autonomy, as well as continual, intrusive questions about personal and family stories, and endless interrogation, including in the most fleeting of encounters, about their reasons for moving to Europe. We learned that the state instituted many practices to ensure that the 'migrant' lived a controlled life, some practices so carefully formalised that they remained invisible to the wider population, some so conspicuous that their purpose seemed to be to advertise the toughness of border control and little more.

> After the sea-crossing we all were very tired. But we were happy to have been rescued. We received food and drink, and were finally able to rest in a normal bed. Then, once being disembarked on an island [Lampedusa], in the coming days we were taken by officials who spoke to us in Italian. No translation. We were brought in a military building and after a while they took our fingerprints with a few words. 'No worry. No worry. Then you're free'. I didn't know that those fingerprints, taken without any consent, would trap me in Italy for many years to come.[1] Those fingerprints made me a migrant? Maybe. But a migrant without the right to move. (Pisa, 24 March 2017)

> From the time that you applied for asylum and from that time straight away then you are treated as a migrant and because then you cannot be doing the things you like because everything must go via the Home Office and you're given the rules. Even if they give you a home where you can stay there are rules in the house. There are rules where you must go to sign on this specific date and at this time. Everything that you do revolves around the Home Office and the time that you get, the allowance that you get weekly, it's also rules from the Home Office so you go to where they tell you and you go at the times they tell you. (Birmingham, 24 February 2017)

When asked to name experiences that made them feel like migrants, one of the most common examples invoked by participants in the UK was the expectation to sign in regularly at an immigration reporting centre (as discussed in Interlude 2). These could be located quite a distance from asylum seekers' place of residence. For example, asylum seekers in Nottingham had to report 21km away in Loughborough, with little flexibility in terms of time, childcare requirements, or planning the most efficient and cost-effective journey.

> It's tough … And if you've got children and they're telling you to be in Loughborough at 1pm and you have to pick your children up at 3:00 that's not possible. (Nottingham, 19 April 2017)

The requirement to sign in at reporting centres was also identified as a symbol of exclusion from British society (as it marked them as being under surveillance where the rest of the population was not). The experience of signing in was also characterised as humiliating, where asylum seekers are stripped of phones and other personal belongings on entry. (Birmingham, 24 February 2017)

For many participants in Italy, the sense of dependency and restrictions on freedom experienced in the reception system has been seen as one of the main aspects of becoming 'migrant', described as a sense of either subtle or intense unease:

> What makes me feel strange is to depend [on the staff of the centre] for almost everything. Food. Clothes. Medicines. Transportation.

> You know? I feel like I became a child again! But I left my home many years ago. I'm not a child any more. I want to buy and cook myself what I want to eat. And I want to decide at what time to eat. (Pisa, 15 May 2017)

These processes of control both organised almost all everyday details of life, leaving only the smallest spaces for autonomy, and worked to isolate residents from each other. The transformation of every aspect of life into something rationed, limited and under threat was extended to suggest that all other residents represented a potential danger to each other. The infantilising process of controlling access to food cupboards, despite the food having been purchased by migrants themselves, is presented as a protective measure against other migrants:

> We can buy our food, but we have to store it in a locked cupboard. The operator [of the centre] has the key and opens the cupboard when it's time to eat. He says, this is to avoid us stealing the food from each other, which I found very strange. (Pisa, 15 May 2017)

This culture of suspicion inculcates fear and distrust, not only towards the state but also towards those who shared similar experiences, and should be regarded as a significant technique of migrantification. The process of containing the complexities of varied lives into the tightly controlled category of 'migrant' involves both practices to set apart the mobile from the supposedly immobile (although, as seen above, our participants challenged these myths of immobility and rootedness) and disciplinary modes designed to disrupt relations of trust both between mobile and 'settled' and among those designated as 'migrants'. The rationale presented for the minutiae of control works to confirm the otherness of the status of 'migrant', sometimes to such an extent that controlled behaviours may continue when formal controls have ended.

> At the beginning, they controlled us when we went out [from the centre], and when we came back. After we asked why, they said that

> the neighbours would not be happy to see too many black people on the street in the evening. Our lawyer said this was not usual, spoke with the operators and they do not control us any more. After this, I don't feel comfortable going out. (Pisa, 15 May 2017)

Asked further to name experiences that made them feel like migrants, one of the most common examples invoked by participants in Italy was the interview at the Asylum Commission:

> During the interview, I had the impression of being at a police office. They were interrogating me. I had the impression they did not trust me. They asked me to repeat and confirm what I was telling [them]. My story, why I had to leave my town and my country. They kept asking me: 'Yes, but could you not just change town if you were not safe in your own? Why did you decide to leave the country? Are there no safe places in your country? Is that possible?' All these questions made me feel like I did something wrong. If they just knew how hard it was to take this decision [to leave]. (Pisa, 15 May 2017)

Living a bare and poor life

Reflecting on their experiences in the Italian reception system as being intrinsic to being made migrants, many participants stressed the same fact: although their basic needs – for food, water, clothing, sleep, health and shelter – were satisfied (albeit at the minimum level), their lives were reduced only to these basic, almost physiological elements of existence. The system was programmed to ensure the simple facts of living, their bare life (Agamben 1995), without any interest in providing them with what makes a good and proper life, in terms of psychological and emotional safety, a sense of belonging, self esteem, self-actualisation.

> Eat and sleep. Eat and sleep. Some TV, some chat with the family and friends outside. Some Italian class. And nothing more. For weeks. For months. Just waiting. Waiting that they call you to the

> 'audition' [in the asylum commission]. I felt trapped. I felt I was losing time. I was losing interest in everything. I was losing my self. (Pisa, 25 July 2017)

This image of existential void and tedium, almost bordering on manufactured depression, is at odds with the pictures produced by the anti-immigrant press of asylum seekers living the good life in five-star hotels, being waited on hand and foot, paid for by the Italian taxpayer, leading to the charge that money should be spent on poor Italian citizens instead. Migrant protests about the poor quality of available food were met with hatred and sarcasm: 'If they are not happy here, they can go back to Africa'. Other protests against overcrowded and very poor living conditions were ignored as if based on exaggerations. Every need going beyond the mere physiological level was dismissed as being 'excessive' and 'pretentious', or as a luxury to which they were not entitled. This was summarised in the motto 'migrants in hotels, Italians in tents', circulated by several right-wing politicians after the tragic earthquakes in Summer 2016 in Central Italy.

According to this anti-immigrant imaginary, there is a limit as to what a migrant, especially an asylum seeker, can desire and have. Migrants are poor and should remain poor. If they have something beyond the bare basic essentials of life, they generate suspicion, evoking the stereotype of the migrant as stealing what they do not deserve. One participant in the UK tellingly mentioned a situation where he was stopped by a policeman, who assumed that as a Black man driving a BMW, he must be a drug dealer rather than the professional that he is – with the means to afford a luxury car (London, 5 March 2017).

Being exposed to the arbitrariness of others

Such accounts of 'migrantification' point to a sense of powerlessness in the face of the arbitrariness of those with the power to detain and deport, seemingly at whim, with no sense of there being any rules or consistent principles to determine whether or not one would be arrested. A misinterpretation of the immigration rules (some participants mentioned Home Office officials who seemed misinformed about asylum seekers' rights), or even an official in a bad mood could potentially lead to arrest, detention and deportation.

Because of this sense of being exposed to the arbitrariness of others, signing in at reporting centres in the UK was described as a frightening experience. It was common knowledge that people could be detained and then deported straight from the reporting centre. One participant described this happening to her brother:

> Whenever you go in to sign in you have this fear, like what if they're going to arrest you, like what happened to my brother when he turned over eighteen, and they told him to go for a sign [in] at the police [station] and one day they just arrested him and they sent him to a [deportation] centre. (Nottingham, 19 April 2017)

Our participants also pointed out the inherent hypocrisy of such arbitrary treatment within a country which claimed to be a defender of human rights on the world stage; they compared it to the authoritarian regimes some of them had fled. This institutional regime of threatening arbitrariness, related to an irregular immigration status, was echoed and, perhaps, emulated in other public services:

> One of the things that even an officer from the council told me, shook my heart, he says, 'I'm not obliged to help you, because you are a person under surveillance. You are a person who has no status.' But even when my application was at the Home Office, they say, 'Even right now, you should get out of my place because I'm going to call the Home Office', so it was so threatening. Then I said, 'I thought the Home Office are there to help you, not as an enemy?' But the way this person was portraying to me, it's like, you have nowhere to go. (Birmingham, 3 March 2017)

Similar experiences were described by Italian participants, complaining of the times they had to go and ask at the local police station about their situation, their permit to stay, the day of their interview at the Asylum Commission, and the common response: 'Well, try and come tomorrow. Maybe we will have some news for you'.

Being nobody

Some experiences of present-day migrantification can be understood, at least in part, as resulting from the outsourcing of immigration controls to businesses, public sector organisations and individual citizens. In Britain, the 2014 and 2016 Immigration Acts aimed to create what Theresa May MP, as former Home Secretary, had called a 'hostile environment' for irregular migrants (JCWI 2016). Through a combination of complicated and confusing rules, increasing fines and the imposition of duties on people who are not trained as immigration officers, the 'hostile environment' reframed the responsibility of public sector workers as preventing those with irregular status from accessing support. These pieces of legislation also normalised the idea of the migrant as someone with contingent access to the welfare state and, in some cases, as someone who must be prevented from accessing public services in order to safeguard them for the deserving in a time of stretched public finances.

Our participants in the UK experienced this in terms of being told explicitly that they had no right to support, as in the interview quote above, but also described in non-verbal communications: downward glances, closed faces or rude looks which gave the impression they were not welcome:

> I try to open an account in a bank so when they came to know that I am asylum seeker by the law, yes by the law I can't open an account but even I could see their impressions at first it is not you are not part of the society here. (Birmingham, 24 February 2017)

> You know, like, when you go to the NHS [National Health Service] and they ask you, like, your personal details and you tell them you're

> an asylum seeker, you get this feeling, you know, like, the vibe changes with the person you're talking to. They immediately look at you down, and they're just, like, 'Oh, he's an asylum seeker, he's nobody', you know. (Birmingham, 3 March 2017)

The processes of everyday bordering have been developed as a means of folding popular hostility into formal processes of immigration control (Yuval-Davis, Wemyss and Cassidy, 2017). Increasingly, we have seen members of civil society tasked with monitoring immigration status and, on occasion, with refusing access to goods or services. In effect, such offloading of bordering responsibility to actors in civil society seems to legitimise anti-migrant racisms, empowering some to act on their aversion to migrants.

> What you are saying about experience I just remember when my mum was here she was going for council property, the way she was being treated the person was like you are trying to obtain this thing you know, looking at you as if you are not someone who is not entitled to have it, they are looking at you as if you are taking something that is ours and all those kinds of things. (Nottingham, 19 April 2017)

The discomfort of continual disrespect of this kind is intensified by physical need, with a failure to demonstrate compliance and to respond to all questions risking access to much needed resources. This sense of being always under suspicion, forced to demonstrate good-will and trustworthiness and entitlement to anyone who asks, was described as another cruelty.

> For example, how are you living, how are you keeping up? And you are not getting any help, and they are not helping you at all, it's like, you owe them your life, or you are obliged to them, they are looking after you so to say, so you need to answer any question that they ask you. It's been very, very hard. (Birmingham, 16 February 2017)

Painful recognition

One of our interviewees, who had been in Britain for more than ten years, described the slow process of realising that the emotional, and sometimes insulting, debate in the popular media and in politics refered to you and your family.

> As soon as I arrived I don't know what's going on, I don't know the culture, I don't know anything about Britain. I slowly start getting into Britain and British culture, you know what I mean. I don't think even in the first year, because in the beginning I am busy, you know, looking for a job. As I have my wife and you know [children] … looking to survive, to live a decent life, things like to find a job, find a decent flat. This was the only thing in my mind, and then slowly, when we start progressing in life, we start thinking 'Oh! There's some issues here' which is the immigration. (London, 1 April 2017)

We are reminded of the strange codes used by the media and political representatives to indicate or inculcate hostility to migrants. For those who have arrived recently, swept up in the urgent challenges of staying alive and providing for their families, this undertone of threat is not altogether comprehensible. The lack of contact between migrants and those deemed 'non-migrant' leaves those who have been displaced without easy or direct access to the consciousness of the so-called majority. If there was, or is, a continuity between the views proclaimed by political representatives or portrayed in the media and the sentiments of non-migrants in their everyday lives, it is all but impossible for those deemed 'migrant' to judge this. Learning to be a migrant also means learning those formal and informal practices of segregation.

> The other issue, to be honest, is … where [I] live, there are not too many English, you know what I mean. So for instance, my first job I worked in, it's not an English company, so most of them are immigrants. So I didn't have direct contact with English people. Some of them they are born here but they are still considered as immigrants. So I start listening and understanding the media and the tone of the media and the difference between the left and the red pages and the *Sun* and the *Guardian* and I start learning English,

> because my English was really bad in the beginning when I came. Even if they were talking about immigration I couldn't understand. If someone was racist I wouldn't get it in the beginning.
>
> I: So it was almost part of your process of integration, understanding how racist it is here? [both laugh]'. (London, 1 April 2017)

Learning to understand yourself as newly positioned in the constructed status of 'migrant' requires this ability to interpret media and political discourse. At least three interviewees had been journalists or media workers at some point in their lives and others were diligent watchers of the media from their home countries and from their new locations. This engagement led people to see themselves refracted through the limited or openly hostile representations of popular media and right-wing political discourse. Our participants spoke in great detail about the constant and endless demands that they prove themselves, told their stories, demonstrated their deservingness and succumbed to whichever doctrine of the 'good migrant' might be circulating at the time. It was well understood that the demand to do more and to demonstrate that you are integrated could never be met.

> Yes, I think everybody sees me as a migrant. From my skin, from my accent. To be honest not too long ago we were talking about it at work and I'm fed up of people telling me 'you need to integrate', so I started to think 'what do we mean by integration?' I need to go to the pub to integrate? OK I accept going with you, but will you come with me on the second day when I asked you to smoke shisha and drink coffee?
>
> He will not come with me on the second day, I know he will not. Because he will feel it is silly stuff blah blah blah do you know what I mean, and we had lots of arguments with my colleagues. To be honest in 10 years I don't have a single English friend. I tried so hard, very hard, seriously. Now I give up. I'm not bothered.
>
> I don't like pubs. I don't drink. I like coffee, I like hot chocolate. My culture is different, my values are different. We can go out, you

> drink your beer, I drink my juice. It is not necessary to drink beer to be integrated. (London, April 2017)

To be a deserving migrant, it was necessary not only to renarrate sad stories of suffering but also to show oneself to be integrated. Yet the positioning as 'migrant' also worked to buoy up the indulged passivity of non-migrants, reinforcing the sense that non-migrants have no responsibilities towards enabling integration. The encounters with the local population described by our participants focused on interactions with particular services or gatekeepers or, on occasion, instances of overt hostility that had stuck in their minds. There was little sense of everyday interactions with non-migrants or of a social world that included many (or any) non-migrants. A member of the Nottingham group spoke of a previous friendship with a neighbour which ended when it was learned that she was seeking asylum. Although the neighbour shared the cultural heritage of our participant, the mention of asylum caused her to cut off the friendship abruptly, perhaps out of a fear that any association with those seeking asylum could destabilise her own claim to be 'settled'.

The process of migrantification combines with other segregating forces, including the oddly patterned population shifts triggered by gentrification and 'white flight' from both residential neighbourhoods and spaces where the informal contacts of social exchange could occur. These overlapping processes contribute to the stage of migrantification characterised by *realisation*, of both the rigidity of the status and the logic of the context in which this status is made and fixed. Somewhat sadly, this included the realisation that the world of the non-migrant would remain distant and mysterious, and the encounters with officialdom standing in as the most notable communications with the 'host society'.

> And the other thing I feel is with the English people, they run away. I hear complaining 'Oh East Ham [a neighbourhood in East London] is full of Pakistanis, Bengalis'. Well, why did you move to Essex? Stay here, live. Keep the community mixed. So, in this case you

will be integrated, I will be integrated, we will learn from each other. But how will we learn if I have no friends, no one to sit with, no one to talk with? And I am talkative.' (London, 1 April 2017)

Not belonging here

Our conversations were marked by a clear sense that state institutions were not there to offer help and support, but to reinforce the feeling of not legitimately belonging to society, leading to a normalisation of discrimination and to a state of perpetual exclusion for those deemed 'migrants'.

This condition was connected to visible symbols of exclusion. For example, participants in the UK mentioned the red doors on housing for asylum seekers in Middlesborough. The red doors had received news coverage after they were defaced with far-right slogans, eggs and excrement, which drew comparisons to both South African Apartheid (Norfolk 2016) and the treatment of the Jews in Nazi Germany (Henderson 2016).

Further experiences of this kind were shared in interviews and memory workshops:

> The day after Brexit, my refuse bin had an inscription in the morning written 'wanker', that was really unfortunate, and then when I reported this to the police, the police were of the feeling that it was just a rabble-rouser, somebody who wanted to create problems in the community. They did not take action. (London, 5 March 2017)

> You get the feeling like you're not going to get the best service or care from [the NHS] just because you're an asylum seeker. (Birmingham, 3 March 2017)

> I have never felt 100 per cent British, because of the way people of my colour have been represented in the media. (London, 5 March 2017)

Explicitly asked about whether they would ever stop being migrants (for example if they took British citizenship), some of the UK participants responded by saying that they would always be perceived as foreigners, using experiences of discrimination that either they or others had experienced as evidence of this:

> You hear about this discrimination even for footballers who have been in this country who are playing every week for big teams in this country and they're still called monkeys, they're still called all sorts of names and these people are celebrities, they are known because they play football and everybody watch them on TV but they still go through this. But they are legally British people already because they play for teams in this country, big teams in the big leagues. (Birmingham, 24 February 2017)

According to her account, one can be the overachieving 'model immigrant' (for example a Premier League footballer) and still be treated as a foreigner. She offers a critique of the call to become an exemplary migrant – a call that is both repeated in popular rhetoric and imagery such as the union-jack-wearing of triumphant sports stars and that has a bureaucratic referent in the tiered visa system, which offers relatively free movement for those with lots of cash or with 'exceptional talent'. The over-arching conclusion is that inclusion is conditional, regardless of what you do or contribute and regardless of formal qualifications for entry. To be marked as 'migrant' is to be confined to this status of being always on probation, with any sense of ease or acceptance vulnerable to being withdrawn at any time.

Distancing

In part the process that we describe here as 'distancing' might be recognised as a version of the so-called burden of representation. People who had been displaced were very conscious of representing 'their' nation or ethnicity or religion. More than this, they complained that they belonged to groups who were tainted by alleged association with violent or criminal or undesirable others. Two women from Nottingham explained this in relation to the murder of Lee Rigby in Woolwich:

> R1: Because a typical case is the Nigerian guy that did the horrible thing, that [murdered] Rigby, the one that … he was born here but everything was not about that, he was from Nigeria.
>
> R2: But there was nothing Nigerian about him, he grew up here, he was a British citizen so, but they still have to link him to Nigeria you know. As long as you are not white they will always want to. Because my daughter was so surprised she was getting a grilling that way, they were saying where are your roots you know. (Nottingham, 19 April 2017)

We may feel that we recognise this framing from earlier accounts of British racism. Certainly, the implication that criminal individuals are regarded as representative of the entire group has been noted before. However, what is being said here is a little more than another complaint about the burden of representation. Our participants raised this case in response to our question: do you ever stop being a 'migrant'? Their response is to point to the conditional belonging that is accorded any perceived 'migrant', including those who are not 'migrants' at all. The point here is not so much that this violent young man comes to represent all Nigerians, despite his (allegedly) limited connection to Nigeria or Nigerian ways of life. What matters is that in the moment of recognising his wrong-doing, he loses any association with Britishness.

This perceptive reading of the structure of popular feeling in relation to national belonging anticipates the creeping practice of citizenship stripping. Without any indication of knowledge about this legal development, our participants recognise the fragility of citizenship 'as long as you are not white' (De Noronha, 2018; Kapoor, 2018).

Being exposed to racist assaults

We conducted our research in a period when the UK and Italian media were full of 'questions' about the movement of people.

Although the UK popular press had been rebuked twice for its role in whipping up anti migrant hatreds (UN News 2015, BBC News 2015a), vilification of those in movement has continued to form a repeated theme in the UK popular and Italian conservative press, a theme amplified in both countries by right-wing politicians. Inevitably, this inescapable wall of resentment and antagonism, visible in every corner shop and supermarket in the newspaper and magazine displays, impacted on how people understood their positioning as 'migrant'.

> For me you know because it is actually in the news, it is everywhere, it has even gone to the subconscious level that you expect it even when you are looking for a job you have this thing that some people have become so paranoid that you want to change your name to something sounding more English. (Nottingham, 19 April 2017)

> Because it is like if they ask your ethnicity to fill in for the demography so they are trying to tell from where you came from and all those kinds of you know demography and generally you know that … especially I don't know what was happening before I came but this wave of anti immigration everywhere, it's as though there is a race in terms of who can be toughest, who can be meanest, who can be … you know … So it feels that way in every experience for me. (Nottingham, 19 April 2017)

Those who participated in our interviews and workshops came from Africa, Asia and the Middle East and, for them, their encounters with native hostility were interpreted (quite easily) as continuations of a wider and longstanding racism.

> R: The situations where you meet up with other people who really treat you as a migrant.
>
> I: What do they do to treat you like a migrant? What sorts of things do they say or do?
>
> R: The behaviours, yes. Sometimes it's difficult to say but even at places where you go, even they're staring, and you think, what

was that about, you know … And there is some negative talking languages and you think, hmm …

I: What kinds of things do people say? Or is it just the look on their face?

R: I remember when I was in Manchester and I met this man and they made these kinds of sounds, you know [makes baboon sounds]. I thought, oh wow. He started chasing me.

I: Was he shouting at you?

R: And making baboon sounds. And he chased me. I was at the park. Walking, I was doing some walking at the park. He even chased me and I felt … I just went to where the cars were and other people. And he went there, back the way, you know, making those baboon sounds. (Birmingham, 3 April 2017).

Those who participated in our interviews and workshops came from Africa, Asia and the Middle East and, for them, their encounters with native hostility were interpreted (quite easily) as continuations of a wider and longstanding racism.

This story moves quickly from the unspoken but apparent aversion displayed towards 'migrants' to a retelling of an experience of overt and threatening racism. We understood from a number of the discussions that the feeling of being regarded as an unwanted migrant often went alongside expressions of racism that were not focused on immigration status. Many of the people who spoke to us recognised that European nations had long histories and deeply established habits of racism that existed independently of more recent anxieties surrounding immigration. The antagonism they faced as 'migrants', therefore, often intersected with other forms of racism. These experiences confirmed again the suspicion that the suffering of people in movement was exacerbated by Europe's enduring unease with its relations to the Global South.

Feeling morally obligated

Before the Decree Law 113/2018, sponsored by former Ministry of Interior Salvini, upon arrival and identification in so-called Hot Spots, asylum seekers in Italy were generally placed in Emergency Reception Centres (CAS), where they should theoretically stay from seven up to thirty days, in order to start the asylum procedure. Applicants without sufficient financial resources could continue to be accommodated in these centres as long as their asylum claim was being processed. This happened if no places were available in the System for the Protection of Asylum Seekers and Refugees, which should provide ordinary reception. The new law draws a strict division between the emergency reception system, just for asylum seekers, and the former system of ordinary reception, reserved to beneficiaries of international protection and unaccompanied minors.

Asylum seekers in Italy are allowed to work after 60 days from their application; however, they lose the right to stay in the reception system if they earn more than 5.824,91 € in the year. In the reception system, they have access to basic services, Italian courses and, in some cases, to legal support. They receive 2,5 € allowance per day for their personal needs. After 2019, the maximum public contribution for supporting the cost of reception has dropped from 35 € to 21 € in 2019.

There has been a long-lasting campaign about the excessive costs of reception, falsely asserting that asylum seekers received 35 € in cash per day. This discourse has become amplified by the effects of enduring austerity measures, with poverty, unemployment and social inequalities rising across the country. As discussed earlier, anti-immigrant media coverage has perpetuated stereotypes about the indolence of migrants, their parasitical role, and the excessive public money spent on refugee accommodation.

These debates provided an effective background for legitimising the legal imposition in February 2017, under the centre-left government, of 'social useful activities' (in other words, workfare) on asylum seekers as a contribution owed to the receiving society. This move has been denounced by many NGOs and by migrants themselves. Our participants saw this as a morally dubious obligation to accept unpaid labour in order to show gratefulness and gain acceptance:

> They [the operators of the centre] said we have to show our willingness to integrate and work as volunteers to clean streets and buildings. So, they said, we would also be kept occupied during the examination of our claim, and people would be more likely to welcome us. I wonder why we cannot work and be paid, like any other, and have to volunteer instead. Do we have the choice? Can we decide what we would like to do? Otherwise, this is like slavery. (Pisa, 30 May 2017)

> I wonder if there is no other work for us other than cleaning streets. We could do many things if they only gave us the choice. (Pisa, 30 May 2017)

Some other participants did not share this view and were more open to 'make a contribution to society in order to be better accepted' (Pisa, 30 May 2017). However, even this acquiescence must be understood in the context of being made a 'migrant', reliant on the tolerance of unpredictable others, always subject to the risk of being excluded again.

Conclusion

The process of migrantification arises alongside the imperial amnesia of Europe. We came to understand this as a form of de-internationalisation, so that European nations erase their longstanding and violent contact with other regions of the world, in the process framing migration to Europe as inexplicable. Our participants in the UK offered many insights into this fantasy of boundedness, including the continuing influence of popular nationalism.

> Because I think it's because people in this country, they also take Britain as the greatest thing that you can ever find in the world. So

> that is why it is called Great Britain so they don't … and the country, to be honest, the country is a good country, so they don't imagine themselves that one day they will also need to get somewhere. So for them this is where they are and this is where they belong. And they are happy with everything that happens here so anything that is outside for them is negative. (Birmingham, 24 February 2017)

This insularity runs alongside an instrumental attitude to other parts of the world, with the rest of the globe of interest only if it represented a threat or an economic opportunity.

> Well, from my personal experience, from what I've seen here, yes. You have to be from, like, that part of the world to know what's going on, but I don't think this country pays much attention to that part of the world.
>
> I: Why not do you think, is it because there is no obvious war or conflict?
>
> R: I think it's just like a, there's no interest there, there's nothing for them there, so they don't really care. That's what I think personally. (Birmingham, 3 March 2017)

One of our participants in Italy made this point more explicitly, calling for Europe to wake up from this imperial amnesia:

> You really wish to stop immigration? Then stop neocolonialism by France and other European countries in Africa. You really wish to stop people dying in the Mediterranean or in the desert? Then provide for legal ways of access to Europe. (Pisa, 30 May 2017)

Notes

1 The participant is referring to the Dublin regulation which only permits asylum claims to be made in the first point of entry and not in other EU countries.

Interlude 4

Telling stories about war differently

This interlude includes a fictional, spoof newspaper created by members of the Women's Cultural Forum during a workshop in Nottingham in 2017. The newspaper is called *The Double Standard*. Working from headlines, and using social media GIFs that were analysed in the media research phase of our project as source material, the group sought to reveal the double standards applied to migrants and to wealthy individuals and powerful corporations.

The first page (figure 7) shadows the 'World News' section of mainstream newspapers, excavating the inter-relationship between past and present Western colonialism and current contexts of corruption and violence in the countries from which people seek protection, of which UK residents often have very little knowledge.

The second page (Figure 8) consists of a spoof of the lifestyle section of mainstream newspapers. 'Life in Handcuffs', as visualised by the group as a mapping of the ways and sites from which migrants in the asylum system are blocked out, was suggested as important contributions to the 'Lifestyle' section of the newspaper, to highlight that while some are concerned with facials and the like, migrants can experience a life barred from even the basic elements of society. Here, instead of the familiar recipes for cucumber facials and dinner party table settings, the section confronts readers with the realities of everyday life in the UK asylum system. The group described this as 'life in handcuffs' due to their exclusion from many aspects of everyday life, such as not being able to work,

AUSTERITY BRITAIN'S favourite single-ply loo paper / Weather for Today: Government will keep pissing on you, and calling it rain / Price: Your Soul (Joking. It's FREE)

LIFE IN HANDCUFFS? LEARN how to SWAG your asylum-seeking status this summer !! Check out the HOTTEST TRENDS and charity shops in our LIFESTYLE section (page 2)

NO HANDCUFFS? LEARN how to SILENCE your COMPLAINING INNER VOICE, keep calm and LET THE REST OF US live in BLISSFULL IGNORANCE! See our BRITISHNESS section (pages 1 to 48)

The Double Standard

OUTRAGE!

MIGRANTS BRIBE GOV'T

(RIOTERS, London) Top executives at Shell knew that money they paid as part of a $1.3bn deal for a huge Nigerian oil field would end up in the hands of a convicted money launderer who awarded the asset to his own company when he was oil minister of the country. In 1998, former oil minister Dan Etete allocated the OPL245 block to Malabu Oil and Gas - a company which he controlled - for a "signature bonus" of just $2m. After years of legal wrangling, Shell and Italian oil major Eni agreed to buy OPL245 in 2011 for a total payment of $1.3bn. The money was paid to the Nigerian government but instead of going to the people of Nigeria, $1.1bn was transferred to Malabu accounts or earmarked for other middlemen. "Etete can smell the money", a Shell senior business advisor, Guy Colegate told Guy Outen, executive VP ...(cont. page 2)

WHY DO YOU ASSUME THAT WE COME HERE TO PLUNDER?

...

BECAUSE THAT'S WHAT WE DID WHEN WE CAME TO YOUR COUNTRY.

SHOCK: MORE HISTORIC EVIDENCE OF BRITISH ENTREPRENEURIALISM & BUSINESS ACUMEN UNEARTHED

"I have travelled across the length and breadth of Africa and I have not seen one person who is a beggar, who is a thief such wealth I have seen in this country, such high moral values, people of such caliber, that I do not think we would ever conquer this country, unless we break the very backbone of this nation, which is her spiritual and cultural heritage and therefore, I propose that we replace her old and ancient education system, her culture, for if the Africans think that all that is foreign and English is good and greater than their own, they will lose their selfesteem, their native culture and they will become what we want them, a truly dominated nation".

Lord Macaulay's Address to the British Parliament on 2nd Feb 1835

2.2.1835

FREE Real Life in the UK QUIZ!

1. What do you do if your neighbour plays loud music every night?

2. What do you need to take care of children?

3. What do the British eat?

4. when you are going out in UK, you need to take:

5. If a British person wants to talk to you should you talk about?

Figure 7: Alternative newspaper, front page, 2017.

and living on £37.75/week. The diagram is a visual representation of this experience. A tagline on 'fashion tips for the discerning asylum seeker' is a sarcastic comment on how migrants are judged on their appearance: too smart, and they are assumed to be sponging off the state (even if the clothes were donated or came from a

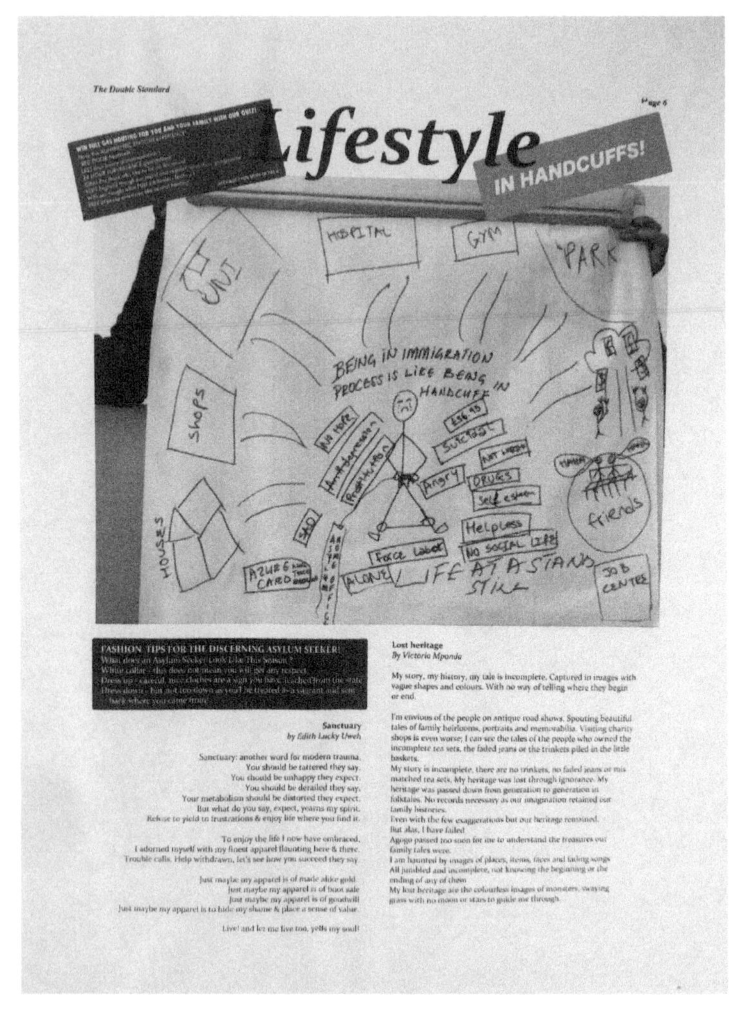

The Double Standard

Page 6

Lifestyle

IN HANDCUFFS!

FASHION TIPS FOR THE DISCERNING ASYLUM SEEKER!

What does an Asylum Seeker Look Like This Season?

White collar - this does not mean you will get any respect.

Dress up - careful, nice clothes are a sign you have leeched from the state

Dress down - but not too down as you'll be treated as a vagrant and sent back where you came from

Sanctuary
by Edith Lucky Uweh

Sanctuary: another word for modern trauma.
You should be tattered they say.
You should be unhappy they expect.
You should be derailed they say.
Your metabolism should be distorted they expect.
But what do you say, expect, yearns my spirit.
Refuse to yield to frustrations & enjoy life where you find it.

To enjoy the life I now have embraced,
I adorned myself with my finest apparel flaunting here & there.
Trouble calls. Help withdrawn, let's see how you succeed they say.

Just maybe my apparel is of made alike gold.
Just maybe my apparel is of boot sale
Just maybe my apparel is of goodwill
Just maybe my apparel is to hide my shame & place a sense of value.

Live! and let me live too, yells my soul!

Lost heritage
By Victoria Mponda

My story, my history, my tale is incomplete. Captured in images with vague shapes and colours. With no way of telling where they begin or end.

I'm envious of the people on antique road shows. Spouting beautiful tales of family heirlooms, portraits and memorabilia. Visiting charity shops is even worse; I can see the tales of the people who owned the incomplete tea sets, the faded jeans or the trinkets piled in the little baskets.
My story is incomplete, there are no trinkets, no faded jeans or mis matched tea sets. My heritage was lost through ignorance. My heritage was passed down from generation to generation in folktales. No records necessary as our imagination retained our family histories.
Even with the few exaggerations but our heritage remained.
But alas, I have failed
Agogo passed too soon for me to understand the treasures our family tales were.
I am haunted by images of places, items, faces and fading songs
All jumbled and incomplete, not knowing the beginning or the ending of any of them
My lost heritage are the colourless images of monsters, swaying grass with no moon or stars to guide me through.

Figure 8: Alternative newspaper, Lifestyle page, 2017.

charity shop); too visibly destitute and 'you'll be treated as a vagrant'. Poems by Edith Lucky Uweh and Victoria Mponda also challenge these expectations of migrants to be figures of suffering, and also, hauntingly, speak to the sense of impermanence pervading everyday life under the asylum system in the UK.

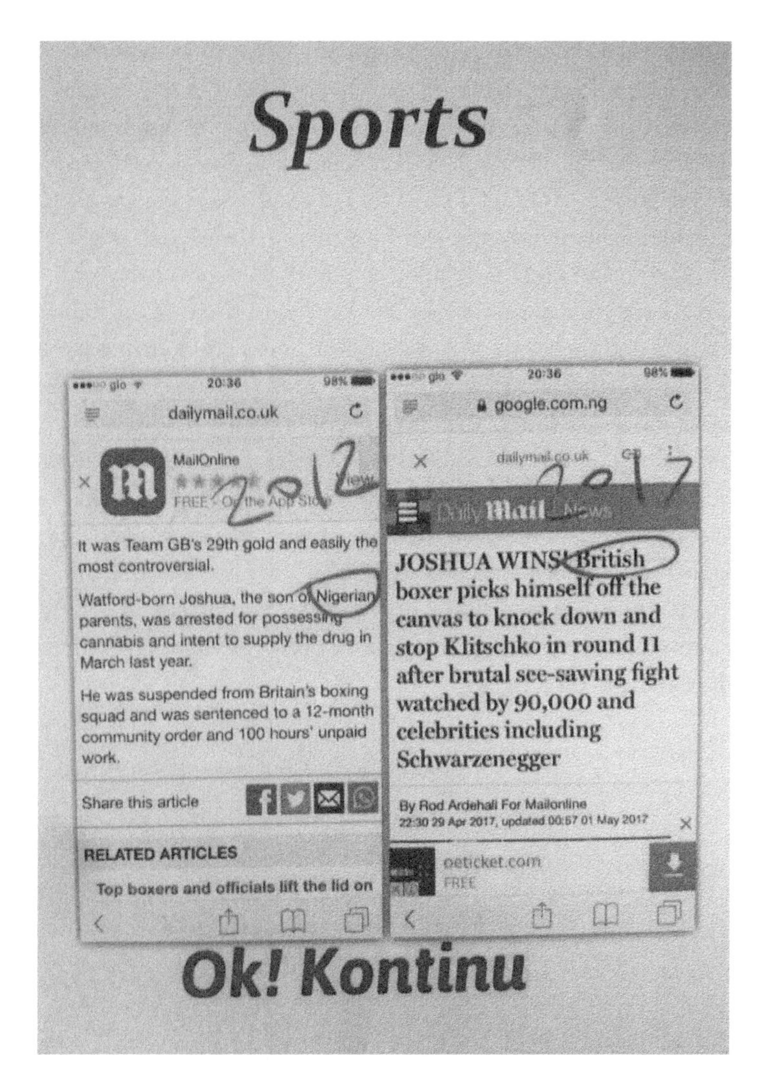

Figure 9: Alternative newspaper, Sports page, 2017.

A third page mimics the popular Sports section which comprises a significant portion of UK newspapers (Figure 9). It draws on a GIF circulated by migrant communities on WhatsApp (discussed in Interlude 2), which contrasts depictions of boxer Anthony Joshua as the 'son of Nigerian parents' in the context of being arrested for cannabis possession but 'British' in the context of a win. Again, this page demonstrates the mechanisms used to 'produce' migrants in a negative light in the British imaginary, and how even British citizens such as Anthony Joshua do not escape harsh judgements. This highlights the degree to which 'here', 'there' and 'migrant' are constructed fickly in relation to perceived national interests.

A fourth page in this process has proven to be more difficult to produce and therefore does not appear here. This fourth page is to be a description of the collectivity and communality that the women in the Women's Cultural Forum bring to the UK, the way that their sophisticated networks of care and support operate in the absence of state resources, and what this might provide in teaching a society more focused on individual success. While the group was committed to telling this story, it was more difficult to imagine how this might be represented within the context of the mainstream press, and so remains an open question for the next phases of the project.

5
Refusing the demand for sad stories

Introduction

This chapter questions mainstream approaches to migrants as tellers of sad stories about their individual migration journeys. With this aim, it introduces performative methods used to de-construct the processes of migrantification through the creation of scenes. We argue that such methods, and the commitments to self-organisation and 'speaking back' that accompanied them, re-position migrants as full and critical participants in collective narrative processes. Within this context, migrants played the role of co-researchers. This indicates a shift in the role of the participants (migrants). In earlier phases of the research, which was focused on media and public narrative analysis, migrant participants responded to research questions set by the research team. However, the final phase of the project was more focused on speaking back to the media and public discourses, meaning that participants were involved in important decisions about the directions of the project. This is methodologically in line with the definition of co-researcher that emerges in the framework of Participatory Action Research, distinguished from other forms of participatory research, because

> from the very beginning of the research, that is, from the moment of design and deciding what to research, why and how, there is participation from the grassroots. Whether it is collective research,

> critical recovery of history, recovery of indigenous knowledge, etc., they participate in every single step of the research process (the research methodologies being user-friendly), in the publication of results and in the 'mainstreaming' of those results. (Fals Borda 1991: 8–9)

We suggest that experiences of persecution, violence, highly dangerous and precarious travels, plus border crossings and arrivals are valuable for our project, but narrations of them must exceed the parameters of individualised testimonials constructed according to the legal-bureaucratic standards of a 'good asylum narrative' or conforming to the media stereotypes of the 'suffering migrant'. The first narrative takes place within the context of the culture of suspicion discussed earlier, where migrants are compelled to tell convincing stories of persecution to prove their deservingness. The second narrative presents migrants as pathetic victims who need to be saved by Western nations. Both narratives undermine the autonomy of migrants and reduce them to stereotypes.

Rather, we suggest that migrants are everyday experts of conflicts and global inequalities, including those that shape the experiences and representation of asylum seekers in the UK and in Italy. The creative, theatrical research strategies we discuss in this chapter sought to analyse the experiences of migrants from a situated perspective (Haraway 1988), while at the same time avoiding victimisation, re-traumatisation and reification of asylum seekers and refugees. The methodologies we used – ethno-drama, critical memory work and participatory theatre – depersonalise experiences and therefore explore collective and social processes that construct the figure of the migrant. By ethnodrama, we mean the adaptation and transformation of ethnographic research data (interview and workshop transcripts, participant observation field-notes, media, documents, statistics, etc.) into a dramatic play-script to be staged as a live, public theatrical performance (Saldaña 2005).

Using everyday stories or counter-memories to disrupt mainstream representations of conflicts and migration processes, co-researchers challenged dominant narratives of the 'suffering migrant'. We also analysed the use of participatory performance processes as a way to shift the frame from the voices of migrants to the listeners of such 'sad stories', in order to provoke reflection on what Gayatri Spivak once described as 'the mechanics of staging' (1992), a mechanics that positions migrants as story-tellers and listeners as judges, saviours, emotional spectators or passive consumers. Where ethno-dramatic processes deconstruct common assumptions about refugee experiences, critically enlightening the role of Western countries in global conflicts and inequalities, modes of presentation drawn from participatory theatre suggest that we need to challenge imperial frames of reception and circulation as much as the stories we tell. The result is an increasingly conscious refusal by migrants of the demand for testimonial as a justification for their existence, vis-à-vis their communities or arrivals and origin as well as in their own eyes (Sayad 1992).

Going beyond the demand for single stories

In 2009, the acclaimed writer Chimamanda Ngozi Adichie spoke of the process of de-humanisation that takes place when people are reduced to a 'single story' (Adichie 2009). The telling of the same story repeatedly condenses complex and singular lives into recognisable sound bites and narrative forms, leaving behind the breadth of experiences – the intricacies and idiosyncrasies that constitute a life. While personal storytelling is often thought of as cathartic or liberatory, and voicing,[1] testimony and self-revelation as somehow on the side of social justice, Ngozi Adichie makes clear that for many, storytelling and self-narration are at best ambivalent and at worst 'dangerous', part of an arsenal of strategies that trap and reify lives into particular modes of speaking them (Adichie 2009). These 'single stories' lend broad-based support for the treatment of migrants as other, transgressive, criminal or suspicious. These stories, solicited under anxiety-ridden conditions, often determine the course of decisions that are literally life and death.

Co-researchers from migrant-led organisations in this project have analysed this tendency in their own lives, describing the consequences of meeting repeated demands from immigration officials to 'tell their story' in ways that are satisfactorily tragic to gain the right to live in the UK or Italy. This requires them to perform the role of victims in front of public officials: stories of fear and victimhood related to persecution, armed or interpersonal violence, trafficking, reduction to slavery-like conditions, highly perilous journeys, losses among family members and friends, and so on, expressed in more or less empathic ways, dominate the rare occasions when people seeking asylum are 'given' voice through NGOs or through first person representation in the media.

Migrants are often asked to tell sad stories to engender public sympathy and a distinction between the sites of *here* (a place of saviour and liberation), and *there* (the place of the tragic), denying the opportunity to analyse and connect the kinds and agents of oppression that move between conflict zones from which they flee and the countries in which they seek asylum. The fact that for many migrants – particularly those seeking asylum – tragedy is and has been a very real dimension of life, does not discount the communicative incarceration that arises from repeated demands to tell only *this* story and not any of the others that constitute their lives. As Ngozi Adichie suggests, it is not always that single stories are false or incorrect i.e. that asylum seekers have *not* experienced hardship or difficulty, but that their endless proliferation locks people on the move in a particular set of assumptions that reinforce policies and everyday practices of exclusion. In this chapter we discuss performative methods which can be used to look at the way in which the public demand for 'migrant stories' – not necessarily sad ones, but sufficient in any case to justify the presence of non-nationals within the Nation – operates as a gate for entry into various social functions, from the immigration system to social settings, but can also be used as a way of speaking back.

Bearing this in mind, it is important to distinguish between forms of storytelling which slot people into closed legal categories and fixed social positions, and other forms of storytelling which are the result of an autonomous need to make sense of experiences and to share them with others, in a dynamic of mutual listening and learning. For Susan Bickford there is a form of 'political listening' which:

> is not primarily a caring or amicable practice, and I emphasize this at the outset because 'listening' tends immediately to evoke ideas of empathy and compassion. We cannot suppose that political actors are sympathetic toward one another in a conflictual context, yet it is precisely the presence of conflict and differences that makes communicative interaction necessary. This communicative interaction – speaking and listening together – does not necessarily resolve or do away with the conflicts that arise from uncertainty, inequality or identity. Rather, it enables political actors to decide democratically how to act in the face of conflict, and to clarify the nature of the conflict at hand. (Bickford 1996: n2)

In fact, stories produced by autonomous, conflictual, 'political' forms of storytelling have the power to shape, reshape, restore, and communicate individual and collective identities (Ochs and Capps 2001). As Jerome Bruner explained, we swim in a sea of stories through which 'we construct a version of ourselves in the world' and through which a given culture provides 'models of identity and agency to its members' (Bruner 1996: xiv). Moreover, as far as they challenge dominant power relations and perspectives, acts of telling and sharing stories become crucial in particular for people on the move (Perry 2007), and may help in creating a less cruel and more liveable world for everyone (Rorty 1989).

Speaking back

Given that the demand for the 'single story' of the migrant emerges not only in the media but from researchers, artists, curators and others theoretically seen to be on 'their side', our project needed to reflexively confront the politics of voicing in both its narrative and material dimensions. The research group in this sense expanded, from those involved directly in the analysis of media and media users trained in sociological methods, to a collaborative engagement with migrant-led advocacy organisations including the Women's Cultural Forum (Nottingham), Birmingham Asylum and Refugee Association, Cantieri Meticci (Bologna) and Implicated Theatre (London). Each of these groups is active in taking back control of the lives and narratives of migrants by engaging in collective processes of support, plus performative analysis of the various circumstances under which the demand for the single story is made. As such, they had articulated aims around changing these narratives through common efforts, but also by retaining the rights and resources associated with storytelling. The Women's Cultural Forum had, most explicitly and independently of our project, cited 'changing media and public perceptions of asylum seekers' as a primary aim of the group for the year in which our collaborative the research was undertaken.

Members of all these groups are at a key vantage point from which to research the possibilities associated with speaking back, changing narratives and understanding the effects of doing so. Rather than accepting the role of migrant as informant, supplier of sad stories, and the role of the researcher as extractor, saviour or profiteer, we aspired to a more reflexive and collaborative process, in which refugee organisers were understood as co-researchers and experts on issues of media and everyday practices of migrantification, and those professionalised as researchers and artists as supporters of this re- working. The 'we' pronoun used in this chapter thus reflects a more complex, transversal (Deleuze and Guattari 2013) and conjunctive (Berardi 2011) relationship between co-researchers, some of whom were engaged with the asylum process and others who were not. Interview material quoted in previous chapters was transcribed and engaged with by co-researchers as source material for the development of counter-narratives. These counter-narratives made use of creative research strategies in order to proliferate other accounts of conflict and asylum seeking than those seen in the media. The first of these strategies drew loosely from practices of ethno-drama. Ethno-drama is a theatrical form that, according to Saldaña (2005, 2), dramatises 'selections of narrative collected through interviews, participant observation, field notes, journal entries, and/or print and media artefacts'.

As with the discussion of the memory workshops in the chapter 4, ethno-drama argues for a more performative and reflexive use of interview and other social research materials (Denzin 1997: 94–95). Other informants of ethno-drama suggest that ethnography be less 'voyeuristic', soliciting material from participants for circulation for academic audiences, and that research materials be 'involved with, committed to, and shared with research participants and a wider public' (McCall, 2000). The benefits of ethno-drama's performative relationship to research for our project were threefold. In the first instance making interview material at once more generalised and more concrete and embodied, such that it could be developed further by interview participants. In the second instance the scripting and scene-ing process made playful use of original transcript material, unsettling fixed meanings such as the narratives of the single story. In the third instance it allowed for material to be translated to local communities and wider audiences.

While Saldaña's definition of ethno-drama focuses on the uniting of the artist (or theatre practitioner) and ethnographer, in our case co-researchers – less convinced of the 'innocence' of either – found ethno-drama to be a useful way to ensure that agency in the research and public story-making process remained in the hands of asylum seekers and refugee participants in the project. In this sense neither the artistic nor the 'ethno(graphic)' in the ethnodrama process were understood as necessarily progressive. Creative and ethnographic processes were re-worked to be in keeping with what Madison (2005) describes as 'critical ethnography' in which questions of the use of research in relation to questions of social justice remain paramount. As mentioned above, our approach to ethno-drama also echoed the commitments of Participatory Action Research in which participants in the research process are no longer subjects of the research but key determining agents, whose interests and desired use dictate the direction of the research outcomes (Fals Borda 1991).

In the UK, material generated by the memory workshops described in chapter 4 – in which co-researchers distilled themes from the interview transcripts into key images or 'scenes', was a crucial first step in our dramatisation process. Rather than scripting interview text, this process of condensation into scenes or gestural images, de-personalised individual testimony to communicate more generalisable tendencies derived through collective analysis, enabling us to explore the experience of migrantification processes. Dislocating the story from the personal worked against the tendency of the sad story which, though formally repetitive, often requires an aura of individual authenticity.

Displacing testimony with a collective analytic process did not mean that the personal was erased but that stories could be placed into a more malleable, adjustable framework that also worked against the re-traumatisation described by co-researchers from migrant-led organisations. In this transition to collective 'scenes' or imagined images, other issues emerged than those dictated by the confines of the single story. It became clear to the research team that collective analysis of the conditions that disable their access from a full life in the UK were more pressing than stories of journeys and the sad stories of the places they had travelled from. Equally, the ways in which these conditions echo and interconnect with the conflicts people have fled came into acute relief.

In Italy, we decided with our co-researchers to work with personal stories, with the risks that this entails (as discussed above). In front of a general audience, we felt that it was important to emphasise the role of people on the move as everyday experts of conflicts, global inequalities and other drivers for migration rather than as providers of victimised testimony or providers of dramatic stories which are intrinsic to the asylum bureaucracy and to the humanitarian self-representation of Italy as a welcoming country. People with migration backgrounds are well positioned to offer insights on how the asylum system really works or on what it means to be 'an eternal migrant' in the new country of residence. The theatrical transformation of their experiences therefore reveals the limit and bias of dominant representations.

Interview texts and transcriptions from the memory workshops exploring how the Italian media represents migrants and their countries of origin was transformed into a five-section script. The script was written together with the co-researchers. It includes monologues, but also fictional dialogues with other 'characters' from everyday life, and imaginary, allegoric dialogues, such as the one between Boubacar and a bowl of spaghetti with tomato sauce (to be discussed later in this chapter). Irony, sarcasm, metaphors, analogies and symbols have been used to stimulate communication through literary strategies and aesthetic effects. The theatrical production, entitled 'Performing memories. Performative reading on media, conflicts and migrations', was performed in Cantieri Meticci's theatrical space in Bologna. All five sections of the script were accompanied by the projection of pictures and excerpts from media press, and the transmission of TV broadcasts, music and other audio materials, selected by the group in order to stress the key points of the counter-narrative.

Stories as relationships

In the UK, some of the first scenes made by members of the research team were derived from their everyday experiences of the demand for single stories. Reading through synthesised transcripts of the interview materials and using key phrases, group members reflected on a number of experiences regarding this demand.

Asked to create a gestural scenario that was then verbalised, the group elaborated a scene that took place at a bus stop. A woman who speaks English as her second language approaches a second woman to ask for directions. The second woman, who speaks English more fluently, does not give directions and instead begins to ask a series of questions, 'Where are you from?', 'How did you get here [to this country]?', 'Why did you come here?', 'What is your story?', 'Do you have a job?'. While posed with relative politeness, the questions continue, and, even though she is running late, the first woman stays to answer them, trapped in the demand for her story (Figure 10). In the feedback session after the scene's performance to other group members, co-researchers described how this experience mapped on to the demand at the border and the bank, as well as in and from the media, as an overwhelming onus placed on the migrant to 'tell her story', in order to access the most basic functions of life and community.

In keeping with Judith Butler's argument in *Giving an Account of Oneself*, the repeated demand for transparent narrations of the 'I' under normative conditions filter, limit and render opaque one's relationship to one's self. Butler critiques this demand for testimony as a way of constructing a 'transparent ethical subject': she suggests

Figure 10: Scene VI: Getting Directions, performed by Implicated Theatre/Women's Cultural Forum, Nottingham Contemporary, July 2017.

that, filtered through a social world that shapes us in ways that are unknowable, this demand holds us impossibly responsible for full self-knowledge and self-revelation and enacts therefore a kind of psychic violence (Butler 2005b). This is doubly the case when, as in the case with refugees, the narration demanded requires re-performances of traumatic events that are often damaging to re-visit, especially when they form the criteria for legal status and basic social acceptance.

This sits on the most dangerous end of what theorist Franco Berardi 'Bifo' describes as 'connective communication': the customary perpetuation of single stories and phrases, which engender disconnected modes of social relation (Berardi 2011: 33). This use of easily repeatable terms and narrative forms perpetuated by media move quickly and smoothly, unhindered by the complex negotiations of inter-related otherness required of grounded and more sensibly oriented kinds of relating. These 'connective' modes of communication disable encounters with difference and otherness to what is already 'known' within white hegemonic culture. Such encounters exist in more committed practices of storytelling, which enable productive engagement with the conflicts and disagreement that are part of working through the legacies of imperial amnesia. Berardi describes encounters in which people work through complexity in conflictual relations as 'conjunctive' (Berardi 2011: 33). The connective communication of the sad or tragic story allows for narratives to move quickly, for the 'migrant' to come to signify something that is understood as a generalised identity, to maintain the imperial amnesia described in the last chapter, and to keep at bay a relationality based in negotiations of difference and one that unsettles this amnesia.

Our project, then, was to work against these tendencies. However, our process did not only have to address the social relations around story-making engendered by the media or encountered in daily life. Early on in the project members of the Women's Cultural Forum detailed the litany of requests they receive to tell their stories to academic studies, art projects, community voicing initiatives and academic engagement strategies, from whom they never hear again. They described the regularity which with stories were extracted from their communities, circulated in realms to which the storytellers rarely have access, and rarely brought back to their communities. Such projects not only ask for traumatic stories to be told repeatedly, bearing the risk of re-traumatisation; they also centre the researcher, artist or NGO as saviour and/or as the translator of sad stories to publics. The extraction of stories thus plays an important role in upholding dominant, hegemonic social positions constituted around the 'migrant' – for researchers, artists, judges, NGO workers as much as journalists and immigration officials. Whilst opportunities within the field of arts and research may exist to complicate and proliferate other kinds of narratives, the question of ownership and the ethics of story-sharing is a key question that emerged in our project. It is not only the demand for single stories, but the treatment of these stories, the conditions of their procurement and their circulation that are at issue for people on the move. Questions about use, ownership and process here are as crucial to explore as the change in narrative itself.

Our attempts to alter the research configuration to a mode in which co-researchers from migrant-led organisations set goals for the projects, made decisions about where and with whom their scenes would be shared and engaged ownership over the material was an attempt to alter the relations they described. This does not mean that inequalities associated with the work were erased. Payment, from which asylum seekers are barred by the UK Home Office, and citizenship status both remained unequally distributed, but the material and cultural resources (and we would hope some of the cultural capital) that emerged through the project are understood to be common assets and any profits directly rendered have been communalised with co-researchers from participating migrant-led organisations. Importantly findings from this stage of the project, and desires generated by the co-researchers from migrant-led groups, are supported by all members of the research team through development of applications for ongoing support of this process.

Still, it is clear that the parameters of funding, the avenues through which it travels, and the injustice of the asylum system generate an un-evenness that sits uncomfortably in the face of even these attempts. Beyond the material relations of the project this aspect of the research was seen less as an 'impact' or outreach activity associated with the research and more of a re-working of other materials generated in other phases of investigation over which migrant organisations had full power of interpretation.

Telling the untold, speaking the unspeakable

In Italy, the dramatisation of ethnographic data from interviews and memory workshops focused on the role that people on the move may play as everyday experts of conflicts in both Italy and in their countries of origin. From this perspective, individual experiences cease to be only individual and assume a more general meaning. Within the context of the theatrical semi-fictional performance, they begin to function as a mirror which reveals what is often absent from Western self-images and dominant narratives on conflict and migration. Through telling the untold, it is possible to challenge the selective media framing of the countries migrants have left and the consequences of those selective frames. Instead of single, sad stories, aimed to provoke compassion, the performance shared news stories which usually do not get into the mainstream media:

> I heard about many other Afghans whose asylum claim has been rejected. Many of them are Hazara. Like me. Not only are we left without interpreters in the Commission for asylum: the point is that our story is almost ignored in Italy [...]. If you are on a bus from Kabul to Kandahar you can be stopped half way by Taliban at a check-point. It may happen that they make only Hazara people get off the bus and then they shoot them, while all the others can continue their journey.

> Did you know? The war in Afghanistan is over! [*He stops and smiles bitterly.*] The truth is: war never ended, you just stopped talking about it. Now everyone talks about more recent conflicts, where global powers are involved, again.
>
> On the *Corriere della Sera*, during the two months around the take of Mosul by Isis, I counted forty-five news articles on Iraq. Well, ten of them were about persecutions and flights of Christian people. No one would deny the importance of this issue. And yet, I feel that it has been over-covered if compared with the complexity of the Iraqi scenario.

Being an expert on conflicts means that migrants can provide commentary on highly complex and controversial issues (which they are rarely given space to do within the mainstream media). This is the case, for instance, of the causes of the rising power of Isis in Iraq. The tone is openly ironic, while the political analysis is necessarily short but well-reasoned:

> At the head of the occupation government, you'll find the viceroy Paul Bremer III. He just had to put his signature on a paper for adopting a new law and abolishing an old one. His first executive order has been the de-Baathification of Iraqi society […]. Unemployment rose after the second executive order of the viceroy, which decided to disband the Iraqi army […]. Emptying the state and disbanding the army makes Iraq an empty space, open to chaos. All kind of militias have crossed the less and less controlled borders with Syria, joining the local ones, Shiites and Sunnis, to fight against the American invader.

The postcolonial innocence and white amnesia explored in the first chapter was also subjected to sarcasm and criticism in many parts of the script, like in the following two excerpts: the first one uses historical references to make the point, while the second one uses a metaphor.

> Eritrea is officially no longer at war since 2001. And yet, in the last seventeen years, two million young people fled the country. On 3

> October 2013, near to Lampedusa, 368 people died in a shipwreck. Do you remember? 360 of them were Eritreans. After that, maybe, media talked a little more about my country, which remains largely unknown. You know a few things about its present. You rapidly forgot about its past, when Eritrea was an Italian colony and the *Ascari*,[2] fuelled by my grand-father's generation, went to die for your flag. As for me, I did not even want to come to Italy: I wanted to go to Australia. Mostly Eritreans want to go to Northern Europe. The fact is that on the way from Eritrea to Northern Europe you find Italy – and the Dublin Treaty. [*He ironically smiles.*]
>
> Imagine: I come to your home and set it on fire. You run away, that's normal. Then, it's your turn to come to my home, where there is no fire. You receive a tent to live and someone says to you: 'You got even too much: shut up and be content!' And then, while you are in the tent and your home is still burning, I make money from you, from your unpaid work, from the bad management of the reception system.

In the Italian performance (Figure 11), migrants do not escape the usual questions of 'why did you leave?' or 'why did you come

Figure 11: Bologna performance, 2017. The image on the screen shows Eritrean conscripts in mandatory national service.

here?' Instead they provide a radical answer which challenges the legacies of old and new colonialism, situating migration as a reaction to colonial dispossession. They also invite the audience to go beyond the simple alternative of welcoming vs. not welcoming people from non- European countries:

> Where we come from, we are used to the fact that life has no value. Take Congo: it is one of the richest countries on Earth, and one of the most plundered. Take Ghana: in a small village of Ghana there is the largest rubbish damp for electronic devices in the whole world. Who cares if local people die? And then, it seems that people are just coming here to take back what has been taken from them in the last 200 years.

The script also provides unique insights on both the decision to leave the country, and experiences with the asylum system in ways that challenge common-sense assumptions about migration. The starting point of these first scenes are the news stories (which received widespread coverage in the Italian media) about asylum seekers refusing to eat the food in the reception centres because of its poor quality. These situations have been exploited by right-wing movements who blame 'fake refugees' for their lack of gratitude and also attack the former centre-left government for spending money on asylum seekers rather than on poor Italian citizens. This is explored in a scene about Boubacar and a bowl of spaghetti.

> The bowl of spaghetti: Did you hear him? He's complaining! What are you complaining about? You have to eat. You have to sleep. Do you know how privileged you are? When you are tired, you sleep. When you are hungry, you eat.
>
> Boubacar: I'm not sleepy. I'm not hungry.
>
> The bowl of spaghetti: Wait, wait. Do not start confusing things: I am the bowl of spaghetti with tomato sauce, and I am delicious. You are the African, and you are hungry.
>
> Boubacar: How can Italians eat spaghetti, morning and evening? It's not good.

> The bowl of spaghetti: Always ready to put us down, are you? Were you not actually fleeing war?
>
> Boubacar: I fled a place where there is no future. I came to a place where the future is not to be seen yet. If I ask about it, they tell me to wait, and wait, and wait. In the meanwhile, another bowl of spaghetti appears.
>
> The bowl of spaghetti: What about just saying 'thank you'!? You might make an effort to show some gratitude. It seems to me like the least you can do.

Other scenes express recurring feelings of regret from migrants, which contradict the common representation of people being enthusiastic to finally reach Europe.

> You know, I spoke with a lot of other young people, telling them the same story. They told me they regret coming here. They would never risk their lives again in the journey. Here, they have freedom, peace, a bowl of spaghetti, but they are alone. You go out and no one talks to you. And this is the thing that even patience can hardly bear.
>
> The journey is terrible. I always feel sick to hear 'Today ten, twenty, 100 people have been disembarked'. People listen to these news stories and worry about numbers. I feel sick because I know what [they] had to deal with to arrive here. My dream is not to see everyone welcomed. My dream is that no one is forced to leave.

Life in handcuffs

Through the dramatisation process, the images described in the memory workshops were developed into theatrical scenes. For example, the phrase 'life in handcuffs' was taken from the interview transcripts and discussions generated in the memory workshops. The group discussed their experiences of being barred from various aspects of British life and the way in which stories often serve as their only currency to be let in or kept out. The group discussed how they might contextualise this image in relation to the media representations of the refugee crisis that we had examined in an earlier phase of the research. In addition to the painting by Prabjot

Kaur (see Interlude 3), the Nottingham group reviewed newspaper headlines around the 'refugee crisis' derived from the media analysis element of the research. The term/image 'Life in Handcuffs' and the surrounding discussions in turn fed into the creation of dramatised scene with the same title. The scene is based on the experience of being 'made' a migrant through practices of exclusion that literally lock asylum seekers out of many aspects of community life and lock them into particular narratives. It was performed silently and predominantly composed of gestures: a woman whose hands are tied walks on the outside of a circle of women holding signs representing key services and experiences in the UK like 'GP, 'Education', 'Community Groups'. She is unable to get into the circle and pleads her case to each person to gain entry. The story here is the only possible option as her hands are literally tied, echoing descriptions of the asylum process of many co-researchers (Figure 12).

Dramatising interview materials through discrete images was useful, not only to de-personalise individual experiences but also in enabling us to explore more fully the ways in which processes

Figure 12: Circle of Exclusion. Workshop image, performed by Implicated Theatre/Women's Cultural Forum, Nottingham Contemporary, July 2017.

of migrantification are often translated non-verbally through gestures and micropolitical events, and the possible resistances to these moments. For example, a scene developed by co-researchers from Birmingham Asylum and Refugee Association (see Scene III in the script at conflictmemorydisplacement.com) also vividly portrayed the gestural dimension of discrimination. The scene depicts a group of students in a further education college studying to become care workers. They are introducing themselves. The atmosphere is light and jovial. After introductions and supportive chatter, a woman in the group reveals that she is seeking asylum. The others make facial gestures, turn away, shift around uncomfortably and otherwise ostracise her without saying a word.

This scene was performed as part of a longer theatrical piece that stitched together different images and texts from the research, including newspaper headlines and collectively constructed scenes and stories. The weaving of less visible, micro-political and gesturally produced moments and highly visible mediatic narratives was, as in the case of the *Double Standard* spoof newspaper, crucial to our analysis of the continuum that operates between the demand for sad stories, and the erasure of histories of conflict and everyday experiences of discrimination (Figure 13).

Implicating the audience into the scene

To move beyond the parameters of a single story, we felt it was important not only to examine the images for the ways in which migrantification processes affected them but to think about how to re-shape these moments and 'speak back'. It was not enough to simply perform materials synthesised by the research, but to think about how, why and where stories circulate. This desire for a performative re-working that not only engaged but implicated audiences and listeners led us to a complimentary dramatisation practice to ethno-drama, that of Forum Theatre. This is a participatory theatre practice within Theatre of the Oppressed, a technique

Figure 13: Installation of media materials on the set of Speak Back!, performed by Implicated Theatre/Women's Cultural Forum, Nottingham Contemporary, July 2017.

developed by Augusto Boal in Brazil in the 1970s. Like the memory workshops it often makes use of 'images', in this case, gestural tableaux or short scenes titled 'forums', which play out moments of oppression, amalgamated from experiences within a group, though not usually presented as 'sad'. In Theatre of the Oppressed, the protagonist is re-framed as the 'hero' rather than a victim and as someone who has agency in changing the situation (Boal 2002).

Beyond performing transcript material, strategies derived from Theatre of the Oppressed supported our desire to interrupt the relational dynamics of the sad story. In Forum Theatre, scenes are played several times so that actors and audience members may enter into the image, take on the role of the protagonist and try to change the dynamics of oppression. The participation of the audience is not in the name of engagement for its own sake but there to, firstly, collectivise experiences of oppression, and engage together in problem solving around possible responses and, secondly, to implicate those who may not see themselves in the problem of changing dynamics of oppression (i.e. the listeners of sad stories). This orientation towards changing narratives and the agencies involved in doing so was as important to the project as changing narrative content.

In the UK, the theatrical element was led by Implicated Theatre, a participatory theatre company that uses Theatre of the Oppressed to engage migrant and non-migrant participants in dramatisations of issues related to the asylum process, labour exploitation and immigration raids on migrant communities. Based in London, they are regularly hosted in the performance strand of Serpentine Galleries and rehearse and perform at Cockpit Theatre, as well as at migrant rights organisations and community centres across the city. Implicated Theatre created their own scenes informed by the research but also supported research groups in Nottingham and Birmingham by workshopping scenes and devising a performance that integrated scenes from all three sites.

The opening scene of the public performance indicated this relationship between agency and the story. In it, people line up to tell their case to Home Office officials, the result of which is either admission to the UK or detention and deportation. A group of actors play the scene, which is then opened to the group. A number of people – both migrant and non-migrant – try to break into the country by telling stories and sharing strategies. Performed both for migrant audiences and more mixed groups, the piece catalyses a discussion about the strategic use of stories (which work and which do not), but also highlight the performative nature of storytelling within border regimes, and what lies beneath this demand i.e. operations of force, incarceration, detention, in short: life in handcuffs.

It is from this framing that the performance proceeds and demands for the story are repeated: a scene at a bank where a woman attempts to get a bank account, and must attempt different narrations to get through (Figure 14); the aforementioned scene at

Figure 14: Scene III: How to Get a Bank Account, performed by Implicated Theatre/Women's Cultural Forum, Nottingham Contemporary, July 2017.

the bus stop where an asylum seeker must tell her story before she can get directions. This accumulation combined with the possibility to 'play' with the construction of the story operated differently for different audiences. When performed within the context of asylum seeker led groups, it lent opportunity to share the story-making survival strategies that enable them to work through and around the system and to release and analyse the conditions they inhabit without the affective labour of re-iterating the (same) sad story and with open acknowledgement that the demand, rather than the story, should be the site of de-construction.

Placing emphasis on the demand for the story rather than on the story itself, however, also implicates listeners (i.e. non-migrants), those who benefit from the imperial amnesia of the mediation story, interrupting their expectations and positions. As participants in the performance, audiences with no direct experience of migration or asylum seeking felt the strain of the relentless demand for the 'sad story'. This rendered the privileges of whiteness and non-migrant status more apparent among those for whom these demands are not made. Through a process akin to what Achille Mbembe has described as 'de-mythologising whiteness', participants described how terms like 'home' and 'migrant' became de-naturalised and their construction by state and media made more apparent. This, in turn, made possible conversations about the complicity and involvement of non-migrants in processes they otherwise deem to be other, and separate from them, and frank discussions about the effects of the constant demand for stories on migrant communities. Speaking back therefore includes both the stories that are told but also the relational context for doing so.

Neither here nor there: 'pedagogies of crossing' and complicity

In what was outlined above, borders between who is understood to be the speaker and the listener, or who creates and responds to the demand for stories was interrupted. The process of imagining and dramatisation developed in this phase of the process also interrupted other kinds of borders. These borders, discussed earlier in this book, exist in the construction of distance between 'here' and 'there'. In the media discourses reviewed, *there* is the (grossly under-analysed) site of conflict from which people must flee ('swarm') to *here*, the site of generosity, liberatory values, and burden to a 'regular' citizenry. The inter-connections between dynamics of oppression that cut across the dichotomy are rarely represented, though they are very present in the lives of asylum seekers. They are what theorist M. Jacqui Alexander describes as 'pedagogies of crossing' (2006): aspects of life and global relations that are seen best from the vantage of those who were forced to move by conditions of global oppression and inequality. Various imaging and dramatisation processes, again drawing from the memory workshops, allowed us to hone in on materials that often humorously took up the proximities between here and there visualised through this pedagogy of crossing.

For border crossers, forces of oppression are often experienced as continuous and colluding, operating *between the here and there* geographies of travel. A scene developed for the final performance makes this very clear. It takes place at the Guinean Embassy, where a person from Guinea seeking asylum in the UK is trying to obtain a passport. The consulate officer quizzes: 'what did you say to the Home Office about why you are here? What did you tell them when you claimed asylum'? Querying whether the person had 'betrayed' their country by claiming political asylum, they suggest that they will 'contact the Home Office directly!' It is not only the power of global elites that move across borders but real and threatened collusions between state authorities.

Telling stories otherwise

There is incredible power and importance in experiential narratives of flight, journey and arrival: both in building the consciousness and knowledge of groups working together to survive the asylum process and in their tactical use in spaces of extreme dehumanisation, like reporting centres. There is, however, a problem in demanding them, even from those with reportedly 'good' intentions.

While it is true, as Audre Lorde says, that 'the transformation of silence into language' is always 'fraught with danger' (Lorde 1984: 42), in the case of many in our research team, the dangers of self-revelation have become obligatory performances. Where migrant stories are offered as a more truthful or sympathetic version of events in media accounts, the consistent demand for sad stories erases the systemic continuities and collusions that produce the migrant. Consistent with the logics of imperial amnesia, the dynamics of voicing that render some as those with a sad story to tell and others the saviours, translators, researchers or reporters who extract, collect and decipher tragic tales, while often well meaning, are experienced as oppressive, and deeply disempowering.

In this project our aim was not to fix the media, to change the story, or to 'empower' migrants, but to analyse and research how these dynamics play out and how we might find other ways to

Figure 15: Final scene of Speak Back!, performed by Implicated Theatre/Women's Cultural Forum, Nottingham Contemporary, July 2017.

communicate – ways that are, in Berardi's words, more conjunctive, unsettling of dominant narratives, and perhaps even disruptive to the smooth operations of ethnographic research (Figure 15). However, our project was limited – in budget, time and capacity – such that we only just began to see the possibilities of a co-research process that takes these worlded accounts as analysis which can be popularly shared, de-constructed, re-worked and tactically oriented by migrant and refugee-led movements. Where we were able to develop humorous approaches within the newspaper, there was much more to do with this aspect of the project that remained difficult to develop in the rawness of dramatising and analysing migrants' experience of life in the UK and in Italy and their interpretations of conflicts around the world. These more refined strategies of storytelling and communication, which encourage both other kinds of representations and other, more humorous and, one might say, human, modes of relating, are the work of the next phases of the process, that both those involved on the project are developing currently. In this the work shifts from more conventional forms of research into the experimental processes outlined in this chapter.

Notes

1 In his book, *Why Voice Matters*, Nick Couldry argues for a 'voice-based politics', in which testimony and voicing are essential to resisting neoliberalism (2010: 12).

2 Eritrean *Ascari* were indigenous soldiers enrolled by the Royal Corps of Colonial Troops of the Italian Army between 1889 and 1941. They fought in the First Italo-Ethiopian War (1895–96), the Italian-Turkish War (1911–12), the Second Italo-Abyssinian War (1935–39) and World War II.

Conclusion: unsettling dominant narratives about migration in a time of flux

We began this project at a time when attitudes towards refugees within Western countries seemed in flux: where official hostility – exemplified by former UK Prime Minister David Cameron's comment about refugees as a 'swarm' (BBC News 2015b) – contrasted with solidarity movements to donate money and practical necessities to refugee camps in Calais and elsewhere. The circulation of the photo of Alan Kurdi seemed pivotal in these shifts in attitude, which in retrospect turned out to be largely temporary, as anti-immigrant politics were quickly reasserted and distrust in media and governance transformed into nationalist populism. As we began our project, this situation provoked many larger questions: why was this specifically being called a 'European refugee crisis'? What were the conditions that were forcing people to leave, and why was there so little information about these conditions?

Whose crisis?

This work arose from our concern about the vilification of migrants in British and Italian media and the apparent lack of news coverage to contextualise situations of conflict and the large-scale displacement of people. We have tried throughout to unsettle the narrative of displaced populations as a crisis for Europe. The language of crisis forms part of the amnesia of Europe. We feel it is a 'crisis' because of a wilful erasure and forgetting of the processes and histories that have led us to this point. Calling it a 'European refugee crisis' also ignores the fact that the nations which currently accept the most refugees are in fact outside of Europe; European countries accept relatively few refugees in comparison.

White amnesia

Our analysis of British and Italian news media confirmed the partial and uneven coverage of global conflict available through mainstream news outlets. The world was depicted largely as a set of opportunities or concerns for 'Western' nations, and for this reason some long and tragic conflicts received little or no news coverage. Instead, wars in other places appeared in mainstream news outlets if they threatened to impact on European business or political interests or if those displaced by conflict might arrive on European soil.

This issue was identified and critiqued by migrant participants in the research project which formed the basis of this book. Those migrating to Britain and Italy were all too aware of the media campaigns vilifying migrants and refugees in these countries. However, they also recognised the wilful forgetting of history that was necessary to maintain the fiction of European innocence and non-involvement. The movement of people could be depicted as a 'crisis', hitting the shores of Europe like a natural disaster, only because the broader context igniting and prolonging conflicts and pushing people to move had been all but removed from popular consciousness and public debate.

Our snapshot of British and Italian media suggests that, in the face of global conflict and events that result in the displacement of people, there remains a strong adherence to ideas of European non-involvement and 'innocence' in relation to global events: that military interventions in other countries are responses to (primarily ethnic or religious) conflict amongst non-European populations, and that European military intervention is about bringing democracy and the rule of law to those regions. This framing of 'innocence' has contributed to legitimising an increasingly securitised and militarised response to populations in movement. The refugee 'crisis' was presented as a threat and catastrophe being faced *by Europe*. In this telling, it was for Europe to decide the reach and limits of international law and responsibility and to decide how *we* should manage *our* borders and the unlucky people washing up there.

Postcolonial innocence and processes of migrantification

We use this term as a way of building on accounts of white amnesia (Hesse 1997). The concerted erasure of the historical links leading to the impoverishment and destabilisation of some regions of the world has allowed European media and policy-makers to present all European actions as benevolent. Even very recent military actions, such as US-UK actions in Iraq, are forgotten or reframed as humanitarianism. In this telling, Europeans and European nations have no *obligations* to those fleeing conflict. Any action that is taken is an outcome of generosity and benevolence and gratitude is demanded. The accusation of 'ingratitude' among refugees and migrants in Italy in particular has become a trope to mobilise racist sentiment and politics.

However, our dialogue with research participants led away from attempting to correct or complete these partial narratives. Simply adding more facts does not dismantle the framework of understanding that views the world as a series of threats and/or opportunities for affluent nations. Similarly, showcasing the 'authentic voices' of those displaced is not enough to dismantle this framework of imperial amnesia and Western benevolence. This question of how to become heard without replaying the objectifying demand to display abjection returned repeatedly in our work. Migrant participants were critical of how little British and Italian populations seemed to know about other parts of the world and linked this very explicitly to the failure to empathise with those displaced by conflict. Participants also wanted to be heard, but not to repeat tragic stories of suffering for the entertainment of others. Throughout the project, this proved a tricky balance to maintain. Inevitably, there are snatches of very painful personal stories here. However, we attempt throughout to keep our focus on the actions of the state, not on the personal narratives of loss and displacement. The outcome is an account of the process of being made into a 'migrant' after arrival, an account that melds together many voices in order to distil the techniques of migrantification. Through the interviews, the images and the theatrical work, participants powerfully articulate the restrictions they face on a regular basis from the asylum system: in the UK, not being able to work or having to sign in at reporting centres; or, in Italy, being stuck in isolated reception centres with little opportunity to participate in society. Beyond these very real practical restrictions, participants also reveal how migrantification operates on an informal and insidious level: being under continual scrutiny, not belonging, being under contradictory pressures to integrate but also to avoid putting down roots. We hope that this focus on the workings of powerful institutions in and on the lives of migrants offers an approach to registering migrant voices that is not objectifying and does not rely on demonstrations of victimhood.

In particular, migrant participants stressed the importance of understanding the movement of people today, including in response to violent conflict, as arising from much longer histories of colonialism and exploitation of the Global South. In direct contradiction to the accounts of mainstream media and politics across Europe, migrant participants pointed to the double standards that allowed (white) Europeans to travel anywhere in the world and be welcomed while jealously guarding their affluence at home, despite the colonial roots of much of that affluence. They also discussed the positioning of some people as 'expats' and others as 'immigrants'. This sense that countries of the Global North behave like absent fathers running from their responsibilities is encapsulated in one visualisation from the group meeting in Birmingham (see Interlude 3 for the image):

> It's like you are in a marriage where the man doesn't want you any more, because you have children with him, but you can see every day that the man doesn't want you but you hope every day that the love will come back.

Changing news about war and conflict

Our project included a survey of younger media users, and was designed to access their approaches to news consumption and attitudes to matters of conflict, international community and migration. Our respondents here demonstrated the very varied forms of news content that inform their view of the world. Although mainstream media platforms such as the BBC continued to feature in their daily news consumption, survey respondents favoured the online versions of such news sources and read across a range of media outlets to 'check' news stories.

Despite the partial and limited representations of global conflict that we found available through mainstream press, our survey of media users showed a very active and wide-ranging collating of news sources as part of everyday audience practice. The distrust towards political institutions and mainstream media that has remade popular politics and participation in both Italy and Britain also seems apparent in attitudes to news coverage. Our survey showed high levels of scepticism and distrust towards mainstream media outlets. However, this did not lead our respondents to turn away from news coverage. Instead, they employed tactics of collating from many sources, cross-checking stories and utilising non-mainstream news sources to build a multi-sourced understanding of current events. Due to this active curation and combining, they felt strongly that they were not 'fooled' by the media. However, at the same time, the energies devoted to becoming better informed despite unsatisfactory and Eurocentric mainstream media did not lead to any sense of empowerment. Our survey respondents felt they were informed but that being informed did not help them to do anything. Instead, they described a media experience of witnessing global horrors but with a sense of helplessness.

Social media and solidarity

Alongside mainstream media depictions of the refugee crisis as a threat or challenge to Europe and European ways of life, social media has played a key role in the political battles over migration in Italy and Britain. This has included, importantly, the media use of migrants themselves. The revelation that refugees and migrants were also highly connected participants in online communities and debates has been used by anti-migrant groups to allege 'non-deservingness' because only the abject should be worthy of assistance. However, we learned that the online media use of migrants played an important role in enabling them to rebuild their lives in a new location and in maintaining connections with both the politics back home and with diasporic communities. What can be lost from accounts of anti-migrant representations in mainstream media is the extent to which migrants are also audiences and critical readers of these texts. Migrants also employed innovative techniques of collation and sharing, in the process maintaining or developing critical collective voices to intervene in the political landscape they had left and also in the one they had entered.

Social media also added an important additional dimension to expressions of solidarity with migrants. For some, we found that solidarity with migrants was marked by a belief in European benevolence, without a deeper appreciation of the history and context that led people to become displaced. However, for other solidarity groups the exchange of usable knowledges in solidarity with migrants, including important information about processes of policing, raids and interviews, presented a more critical media forum. Although the collecting of material aid was the focus of most of the online solidarity that we examined, the shift into a more politicised solidarity that challenged state practices was visible in some groups, revealing, at the same time, some challenges to postcolonial amnesia and assumed innocence.

These alternative narratives via social media reflect a climate of suspicion towards 'official sources'. For solidarity movements, this suspicion was directed towards the hostility from mainstream media and politicians, as both gave official sanctioning to anti-immigrant views. Predictably, this culture of suspicion also fuelled anti-migrant activity via social media. In particular, the circulation of conspiracy theories with partial information or reinterpreted aspects of mainstream news played a significant role in creating online communities of distrust united by anti-migrant racism. More generally, there are questions to be asked about the role of social media as the property of tech giants, which are not democratically accountable, and which have recently been controversial in terms of their role undermining democratic processes and stoking hate speech. The fact that migrants were forced to rely on these platforms for support and information underlines the absence of safe and legal means of travel, and the lack of reliable advice for navigating a cruel and impenetrable immigration system.

Overall, our project demonstrates the need to consider a range of media practices when examining the role of media in the politics of migration. The differing media audiences that we analyse – new media users, migrants, migrant solidarity activists and anti-migrant activists – show the extent to which media audiences are adopting increasingly multi-sourced approaches to news consumption.

Not telling sad stories

The process of seeking asylum or regularised immigration status demands a display of distress. This telling of sad stories of migration is central to the process of demonstrating deservingness, yet it is also an aspect of the dehumanising limitations placed on migrants.

Displaying personal pain through repetition of the sad story of migration has become a demand linking hostile or sceptical receiving communities and those administering official processes.

To unsettle this practice, we sought to go beyond the single stories (as critiqued by Ngozi Adichie). Employing techniques from Theatre of the Oppressed, we worked collectively to create theatricalised and analytic 'stories' that illuminated the power relations of migration and migrant experience. Through the use of techniques developed through political theatre, we refused any pretence that it was empowering to demand that people performed their sad stories. Instead, we worked together to devise approaches to telling stories otherwise.

Solidarities and critical questions in a changing landscape

Over the few years from the start of the research project to the writing of this book, the European political landscape has continued to shift. The UK has seen the Brexit vote and, in its aftermath, increasingly divisive politics, within which anti-immigrant views have played a central role. In 2018, the mechanisms of the hostile environment caused a number of British citizens of former colonies to be detained, made destitute and, in some cases, deported (in what became termed the 'Windrush Scandal'[1]) – underlining that even British citizenship offers no protection against the techniques of migrantification. In Italy, the election of the right-wing government was in part due to distrust in how the asylum process for people crossing the Mediterranean was being managed, including conspiracy theories about NGOs colluding with organised crime networks. The withdrawal of support structures and policies criminalising solidarity with migrants soon followed.

As the situation unfolds, questions of international responsibility and the role of the media in covering global conflicts (as well as those who flee them) will continue to be central to how we respond. There is a more urgent question about how we build networks of solidarity which will challenge white amnesia and presumed European innocence, particularly at a time when powerful state actors and media commentators are denying any Western responsibility for global conflicts and connecting this to populist grievances. We hope that our book offers some resources for thinking of these questions differently, and considering how such solidarities might be built.

Notes

1 The term 'Windrush' refers to the *Empire Windrush*, a ship which brought large numbers of Caribbean migrants to the UK in 1948; it also refers to migrants who settled in the UK during this period and who are called the 'Windrush Generation'.

Bibliography

P. Achter (2008) 'Comedy in Unfunny Times: News Parody and Carnival After 9/11', *Critical Studies in Media Communication*, 25:3, pp. 274–303.

C. Adichie (2009) 'The danger of a single story, *TEDGlobal* (July), https://www.ted.com/talks/chimamanda_adichie_the_danger_of_a_single_story/transcript. Accessed 1 November 2018.

G. Agamben (1995) *Homo Sacer: Sovereign Power and Bare Life* (Stanford, CA: Stanford University Press).

G. Agamben (2005) *States of Exception* (Chicago: University of Chicago Press).

AGCOM (2018) *Italiani alla fonte. Come, quando e dove ci informiamo* (Milan: Egea).

M. J. Alexander (2006) *Pedagogies of Crossing: Meditations on Feminism, Sexual Politics, Memory, and the Sacred* (Durham, NC: Duke University Press).

Amnesty International (2016) *Hotspot Italy: How EU's Flagship Approach Leads To Violations of Refugee And Migrant Rights*, Amnesty International (November 2016).

A. Anastasi, A. Raffa and M. Fenris (2018) 'Sondaggi politici Piepoli: chiusura porti e Ong, Salvini raccoglie un plebiscito', *BlastingNews* (25 June), https://it.blastingnews.com/politica/2018/06/sondaggi-politici-piepoli-chiusura-porti-e-ong-salvini-raccoglie-un-plebiscito-002638219.html. Accessed 15 October 2018.

B. Anderson (2014) *Us vs Them: The Dangerous Politics of Immigration Control* (Oxford: Oxford University Press).

I. Arreguín-Toft (2001) 'How the Weak Win Wars: A Theory of Asymmetric Conflict', *International Security*, 26:1, pp. 93–128.

V. Bachmann, and J.D. Sidaway (2016) 'Brexit Geopolitics', *Geoforum*, 77, pp. 47–50.

Baobab Experience, 'About us', https://baobabexperience.org/. Accessed 5 November 2018.

J. Baudrillard (1991) *The Gulf War Did Not Take Place* (Bloomington, IN: Indianapolis University Press).

Bibliography

BBC News (2015a) 'Tackle tabloid "hate speech", UN commissioner urges UK', *BBC News* (24 April), https://www.bbc.co.uk/news/uk-32446673. Accessed 12 November 2018.

BBC News (2015b) 'David Cameron criticised over migrant "swarm" language', *BBC News* (30 July), https://www.bbc.co.uk/news/uk-politics-33716501. Accessed 20 May 2019.

F. Berardi (2011) *After the Future* (Edinburgh: AK Press).

M. Berry, I. Garcia-Blanco and K. Moore (2016) 'Press coverage of the refugee and migrant crisis in the EU: A content analysis of five European countries', UNHCR, http://www.unhcr.org/56bb369c9.html. Accessed 1 November 2018.

M. Bhatia, S. Poynting and W. Tufail (eds) (2018) *Media, Crime and Racism* (Houndmills: Palgrave Macmillan).

S. Bickford (1996) *The Dissonance of Democracy: Listening, Conflict and Citizenship* (Ithaca and London: Cornell University Press).

S. Blinder and L. Richards (2018) 'UK Public opinion towards immigration: overall attitudes and level of concern'. *Migration Observatory* briefing (7 June), https://migrationobservatory.ox.ac.uk/wp-content/uploads/2016/04/BRIEFING-Public-Opinion-pdf.pdf. Accessed 30 September 2019.

A. Boal (2002) *Theatre of the Oppressed* (London: Pluto Press).

P. J. Boczkowski and Z. Papacharissi (eds) (2018) *Trump and the Media* (Cambridge, Mass: MIT Press).

C. Brambilla (2014) 'Shifting Italy/Libya Borderscapes at the Interface of EU/Africa Borderland: A "Genealogical" Outlook from the Colonial Era to Postcolonial Scenarios', *ACME: An International E-Journal for Critical Geographies*, 13:2, pp. 220–245.

W. Brown (2010) *Walled States, Waning Sovereignty* (Cambridge, MA: MIT Press).

J. Bruner (1996) *The Culture of Education* (Cambridge, MA: Harvard University Press).

S. Burg and P. Shoup (eds) (2000) *Ethnic Conflict and International Intervention: Crisis in Bosnia-Herzegovina, 1990–93* (Abingdon: Routledge).

J. Butler (2004) *Precarious Life: The Powers of Mourning and Violence* (London: Verso).

J. Butler (2005a) 'Photography, War, Outrage', *PMLA*, 20:3 (May 2005), pp. 822–827.

J. Butler (2005b) *Giving an Account of Oneself* (New York: Fordham University Press).

J. Butler (2009) *Frames of War: When Is Life Grievable?* (New York: Verso Books).

G. P. Calchi Novati (2008) 'Italy and Africa: How to Forget Colonialism', *Journal of Modern Italian Studies*, 13:1, pp. 327–356.

G. Capitani (2016) *Rights Denied*, Oxfam (22 June), https://d1tn3vj7xz9fdh.cloudfront.net/s3fs-public/file_attachments/bp-hotspots-migrants-italy-220616-en.pdf. Accessed 10 September 2018.

Carta di Roma (2015) *Notizie di confine. Terzo Rapporto Carta di Roma 2015* (December), https://www.cartadiroma.org/wp-content/uploads/2015/12/Rapporto-2015_-cartadiroma.pdf. Accessed 1 November 2018.

Carta di Roma (2017) 'Navigare a vista, il racconto delle operazioni di ricerca e soccorso di migranti nel Mediterraneo centrale', *Carta di Roma* (24 May), https://www.cartadiroma.org/news/cospe-ricerca-soccorso-migranti-mediterraneo-centrale/. Accessed 10 November 2018.

Centre for Economics and Business Research (2017) *CEBR Special Report: Economic Costs of Limiting Immigration* (24 May), https://cebr.com/reports/cebr-special-report-economic-consequences-of-limiting-migration/. Accessed 10 October 2018.

M. de Certeau (2011) *The Practice of Everyday Life* (Berkeley: University of California Press).

T. Cherkaoui (2017) *The News Media at War: The Clash of Western and Arab Networks in the Middle East* (London-New York: I.B. Tauris).

B. Chimni (1998) 'The Geopolitics of Refugee Studies: A View from the South', *Journal of Refugee Studies*, 11:4, pp. 350–374.

L. Chouliaraki, M. Georgiou and R. Zaborowski (2017) *The European 'Migration Crisis' and the Media: A Cross-European Press Content Analysis* (London: LSE).

I. Cobain (2015) 'Cooperation between British spies and Gaddafi's Libya revealed in official papers', *Guardian* (22 January), https://www.theguardian.com/uk-news/2015/jan/22/cooperation-british-spies-gaddafi-libya-revealed-official-papers. Accessed 10 November 2018.

C. Coker (2004) *The Future of War: The Re-Enchantment of war in the Twenty-First Century* (Malden: Blackwell).

Corriere della Sera (2015) 'Baobab, chiude il centro migranti. I volontari preparano la resistenza', Rome Edition (6 December), https://roma.corriere.it/notizie/cronaca/15_dicembre_06/centro-baobab-no-sgombero-volontari-preparano-resistenza-a7d0dcac-9c16-11e5-9b09-66958594e7c5.shtml. Accessed 10 November 2018.

N. Couldry (2010) *Why Voice Matters: Culture and Politics After Neoliberalism* (London: SAGE).

S. Critchley (2002) *On Humour* (Abingdon: Routledge).

P. Cuttitta (2014) '"Borderizing" the Island Setting and Narratives of the Lampedusa "Border Play"', *ACME: An International E-Journal for Critical Geographies*, 13:2, pp. 196–219.

P. Cuttitta (2018) 'Delocalization, Humanitarianism, and Human Rights: The Mediterranean Border Between Exclusion and Inclusion', *Antipode*, 50:3, pp. 783–803.

I. Danewid (2017) 'White Innocence and the Black Mediterranean: Hospitality and the Erasure of History', *Third World Quarterly*, 38:7, pp. 1674–1689.

J. Daniels (2009) *Cyber Racism: White Supremacy Online and the New Attack on Civil Rights* (New York: Rowman & Littlefield).

Bibliography

J. Daniels (2013) 'Race and Racism in Internet Studies: A Review and Critique', *New Media & Society*, 15:5, pp. 695–719.

G. Debord (1967) *Society of the Spectacle* (London: Rebel Press).

A. Del Boca (1984) *Gli italiani in Africa Orientale IV. Nostalgia delle colonie* (Rome-Bari: Laterza).

A. Del Boca (2005) *Italiani, brava gente?* (Vicenza: Neri Pozza).

G. Deleuze and F. Guattari (2013) *A Thousand Plateaus: Capitalism and Schizophrenia* (London: Bloomsbury Press).

N. Denzin (1997) *Interpretive Ethnography: Ethnographic Practices for the 21st Century* (London: SAGE).

P. Doboš (2019) 'The Problem of Different Postcolonial Spatial Contexts in Television News About Distant Wartime Suffering', *International Communication Gazette*, pp. 1–20.

M. Douglas (2002) *Purity and Danger: An Analysis of Concepts of Pollution and Taboo* (Abingdon: Routledge).

Drudi, E. and M. Omizzolo (2015) '"Ciò che mi spezza il cuore". Eritrea: dalla grande speranza alla grande delusione', in M. Omizzolo and P. Sodano, *Migranti e territori. Lavoro, diritti, accoglienza* (Rome: Ediesse), pp. 399–446.

ECRE et al. (2016) 'The implementation of the hotspots in Italy and Greece', *European Council on Exiles and Refugees* (December), https://www.ecre.org/wp-content/uploads/2016/12/HOTSPOTS-Report-5.12.2016.pdf. Accessed 10 November 2018.

N. El-Enany (2016) 'Aylan Kurdi: The Human Refugee', *Law and Critique*, 27:1, pp. 13–15.

M. Ekman (2014) The Dark Side of Online Activism: Swedish Right-Wing Extremist Video Activism on YouTube', *MidieKultur*, 30, pp. 79–99.

M. Ekman (2018) 'Anti-Refugee Mobilisation in Social Media: The Case of Soldiers of Odin', *Social Media + Society* (January–March), pp. 1–11.

J. Ellis (2000) *Seeing Things: Television in the Age of Uncertainty* (London: I.B. Tauris).

J. Ellis (2009a) 'What Are We Expected to Feel? Witness, Textuality and the Audiovisual', *Screen* 50:1, pp. 67–76.

J. Ellis (2009b) 'Mundane Witness', in P. Frosh and A. Minchevski (eds), *Media Witnessing: Testimony in the Age of Mass Communication* (Basingstoke: Palgrave Macmillan), pp. 73–88.

European Commission (2018) 'Managing migration: Commission expands on disembarkation and controlled centre concepts', *European Commission Press Release Database* (24 July), http://europa.eu/rapid/press-release_IP-18-4629_en.htm. Accessed 10 November 2018.

O. Fals Borda (1991) 'Some Basic Ingredients', in O. Fals Borda and M. Anisur Rahman (eds), *Action and Knowledge: Breaking the Monopoly with Participatory Action Research* (New York: The Apex Press), pp. 8–9.

L. Fang (2018) 'John Bolton chairs an actual "fake news" publisher infamous for spreading anti-Muslim hate', *The Intercept* (23 March), https://theintercept.com/2018/03/23/gatestone-institute-john-bolton-chairs-an-actual-fake-news-publisher-infamous-for-spreading-anti-muslim-hate/. Accessed 1 November 2018.

F. Fanon (1986) *Black Skin, White Masks* (London: Pluto Press).

J. Farkas, J. Schou and C. Neumayer (2018) 'Platformed Antagonism: Racist Discourses on Fake Muslim Facebook Pages', *Critical Discourse Studies*, 15:5, pp. 463–480.

Il Fatto Quotidiano (2018) 'Missione in Niger, la Camera dà l'ok. FI e Fdi votano a favore, contrari LeU e M5s "Interessi neocoloniali rischiosi per Italia"', *Il Fatto Quotidiano* (17 January), https://www.ilfattoquotidiano.it/2018/01/17/missione-in-niger-la-camera-da-lok-fi-e-fdi-votano-a-favore-contrari-leu-e-m5s-interessi-neocoloniali-rischiosi-per-italia/4098971/. Accessed 10 November 2018.

L. Fekete (2001) 'The Emergence of Xeno-Racism', *Race and Class*, 43:2 (October 2001), pp. 23–40.

Filiera Sporca (2016) 'La raccolta dei rifugiati. Trasparenza di filiera e responsabilità sociale delle aziende', *Filiera Sporca*, http://www.filierasporca.org/2016/wp-content/uploads/2016/06/filierasporca_2016.pdf. Accessed 6 January 2020.

E. Fletcher (2008) 'Changing Support for Asylum Seekers: An Analysis of Legislation and Parliamentary Debates', *Sussex Centre for Migration Research Working Paper* #49.

R. Fletcher, and R. K. Nielsen (2018) 'Generalised Scepticism: How People Navigate News on Social Media', *Information, Communication & Society*, 3:20, pp. 1–19.

Forensic Oceanography & Watch the Med (2016) 'Death by rescue, the lethal effects of the EU's policies of non-assistance at sea', https://deathbyrescue.org/. Accessed 1 November 2018.

J. Galtung (2002) 'Peace Journalism – A Challenge', in W. Kempf and H. Luostarinen (eds), *Journalism and the New World Order, Vol. II, Studying War and the Media* (Goteborg: Nordicom), pp. 259–272.

J. Galtung, and M. H. Ruge (1965) 'The Structure of Foreign News: The Presentation of the Congo, Cuba and Cyprus Crises in Four Norwegian Newspapers', *Journal of Peace Research*, 2:1, pp. 64–91.

Gatestone Institute (2018) 'About us', Gatestone Institute, https://www.gatestoneinstitute.org/about/. Accessed 10 November 2018.

N. De Genova (2016a) 'The "Crisis" of the European Border Regime: Towards a Marxist Theory of Borders', *International Socialism: A Quarterly Review of Socialist Theory*, 150, http://isj.org.uk/the-crisis-of-the-european-border-regime-towards-a-marxist-theory-of-borders/. Accessed 12 November 2018.

N. De Genova (2016b) 'The "European" Question: Migration, Race, and Postcoloniality in "Europe"', in A. Amelina, K. Horvath and B. Meeus

(eds), *An Anthology of Migration and Social Transformation: European Perspectives* (Berlin: Springer), pp. 343–356.
N. De Genova, S. Mezzadra and J. Pickles (2014) 'New Keywords: Migration and Borders', *Cultural Studies*, 29:1, pp. 55–87.
C. Gentry and A. Eckert (eds) (2014) *The Future of Just War: New Critical Essays* (Athens, GA/London: University of Georgia Press).
M. Georgiou and R. Zaborowski (2017) 'Media coverage of the "refugee crisis": a cross-European Perspective', *Council of Europe*, https://edoc.coe.int/en/refugees/7367-media-coverage-of-the-refugee-crisis-a-cross-european-perspective.html. Accessed 1 November 2018.
E. Gilboa (2005) 'The CNN Effect: The Search for a Communication Theory of International Relations', *Political Communication*, 22:1, pp. 27–44.
P. Gilroy (2004) *After Empire: Melancholia or Convivial Culture* (Abingdon: Routledge).
W. Goodman (1992) 'Somalia: How Much Did TV Shape Policy?', *New York Times* (8 December 1992).
S. Goodman and S. Speer (2007) 'Category Use in the Construction of Asylum Seekers', *Critical Discourse Studies*, 4:2, pp. 165–185.
J. Gordon, P. Rowinski and G. Stewart (eds) (2013) *Br(e)aking the News: Journalism, Politics and New Media* (Oxford: Peter Lang).
J. Gray, J. Jones and E. Thompson (2009) *Satire TV: Politics and Comedy in the Post-Network Era* (New York: NYU Press).
M. Griffin (2004) 'Picturing America's "War on Terrorism", in Afghanistan and Iraq: Photographic Motifs as News Frames', *Journalism*, 5:4, pp. 381–402.
F. Grignetti (2016) '"Uomini dell'Isis dietro i flussi dei migranti dalla Libia"', *La Stampa* (4 August), https://www.lastampa.it/2016/08/04/italia/uomini-dellisis-dietro-i-flussi-dei-migranti-dalla-libia-IzihUagr92IqBfUZkLEoNI/pagina.html. Accessed 1 November 2018.
GuardianWitness (2015) 'Outside looking in: what's it like to be Eritrean living abroad?', *Guardian* (27 July), https://www.theguardian.com/world/2015/jul/27/eritrean-diaspora-share-your-experiences. Accessed 10 November 2018.
M. Guerzoni (2018) 'Salvini, l'ira del ministro sotto assedio: è una montatura, vogliono screditarci', *Corriere della Sera* (17 July), https://www.corriere.it/politica/18_luglio_18/ira-leader-leghista-sotto-assedio-0879d5ec-89fc-11e8-8bbc-b107b233a106.shtml. Accessed 2 September 2018.
J. Habermas (2006) *The Divided West* (Cambridge: Polity Press).
G. Hage (2016) 'Etat de siège: A Dying Domesticating Colonialism?' *American Ethnologist*, 43:1, pp. 38–49.
G. Hage (2017) *Is Racism an Environmental Threat?* (Cambridge: Polity Press).
D. Hallin (1989) *The 'Uncensored War': The Media and Vietnam* (Berkeley: University of California Press).
D. Haraway (1988) 'Situated Knowledges: The Science Question in Feminism and the Privilege of Partial Perspective', *Feminist Studies*, 14:3, pp. 575–599.

L. Harbom and P. Wallensteen (2007) 'Armed Conflict, 1989–2006', *Journal of Peace Research* 44:5, pp. 623–634.

R. Harris (1983) *Gotcha! The Media, the Government and the Falklands Crisis* (London: Faber and Faber).

A. Hartnell (2010) 'W.E.B. Du Bois, William Faulkner, and the dialectic of Black and White: In Search of Exodus for a Postcolonial American South', *Callaloo*, 33:2, pp. 521–536.

F. Haug (1992) *Beyond Female Masochism: Memory-Work and Politics* (London: Verso).

V. Hawkins (2011) 'Media Selectivity and the Other Side of the CNN Effect: The Consequences of Not Paying Attention to Conflict', *Media, War & Conflict*, 4:1, pp. 55–68.

E. Henderson (2016) 'Asylum seekers in Middlesbrough suffering abuse after front doors were painted red to identify them will have doors repainted', *Independent* (20 January), https://www.independent.co.uk/news/uk/home-news/home-office-investigation-launched-after-asylum-seekers-in-middlesbrough-claim-doors-were-painted-a6822211.html. Accessed 30 September 2016.

A. Hern (2019) 'Older people more likely to share fake news on Facebook, study finds', *Guardian* (10 January), https://www.theguardian.com/technology/2019/jan/10/older-people-more-likely-to-share-fake-news-on-facebook. Accessed 15 April 2019.

B. Hesse (1997) 'White Governmentality: Urbanism, Nationalism, Racism', in S. Westwood and J. Williams (eds), *Imagining Cities: Scripts, Signs, Memories* (Abingdon: Routledge), pp. 86–103.

M. Holehouse (2015) 'EU Chief: Migrant Influx is "Campaign of Hybrid Warfare" by Neighbours to Force Concessions', *The Telegraph* (6 October), www.telegraph.co.uk/news/worldnews/europe/eu/11915798/EU-chief-Migrant-influxis-campaign-of-hybrid-warfare-by-neighbours-to-force-concessions.html. Accessed 1 November 2018.

Huffington Post (2017) 'Sondaggio Ixé per Agorà: per il 48% il "aiutiamoli a casa loro" di Renzi (e Salvini) è un'espressione di buon senso', *Huffington Post* (7 July), https://www.huffingtonpost.it/2017/07/21/sondaggio-ixe-per-agora-per-il-48-il-aiutiamoli-a-casa-loro_a_23040779/. Accessed 1 November 2018.

N. Huntermann (2009) *Joystick Soldiers: The Politics of Play in Military Video* (Abingdon: Routledge).

S. Huntington (1996) *The Clash of Civilisations and the Remaking of the World Order* (New York: Simon and Schuster).

Il Tempo (2014) 'Così i veterani della guerra in Siria tornano peI r combattere l'Europa', *Il Tempo* (27 July), https://www.iltempo.it/cronache/2014/07/27/news/cosi-i-veterani-della-guerra-in-siria-tornano-per-combattere-leuropa-949340/. Accessed 1 November 2018.

Il Tempo (2015) 'La denuncia di Eurojust: miliziani dell'Isis nascosti sui barconi degli immigrati, Il Tempo (7 July), https://www.iltempo.it/esteri/2015/07/07/news/la-denuncia-di-eurojust-miliziani-dell-isis-nascosti-sui-barconi-degli-immigrati-981788/. Accessed 10 November 2018.

B. Jahn (2012) 'Humanitarian Intervention – What's in a Name?', *International Politics*, 49:1, pp. 36–58.

JCWI (2016) 'What's next for the hostile environment: the 2016 Immigration Act and the Queen's Speech', Joint Council for the Welfare of Immigrants (23 May), https://jcwi.org.uk/blog/2016/05/23/what%E2%80%99s-next-hostile-environment-immigration-act-2016-and-queen%E2%80%99s-speech. Accessed 30 September 2016.

A. Juhász, C. Molnár and E. Zgut (2017) *Refugees, Asylum and Migration Issues in Hungary* (Prague: Heinrich-Böll-Stiftung).

M. Kaldor (2012) *Old and New Wars: Organised Violence in a Global Era* (Cambridge: Polity).

M. Kaldor (2013) 'In Defence of New Wars', *Stability*, 2 (1):4, pp. 1–16.

S. Kalyvas (2001) 'New and Old Civil Wars: A Valid Distinction?' *World Politics*, 54, pp. 99–118.

N. Kapoor (2018) *Deport, Deprive, Extradite: 21st Century Extremism* (London: Verso).

E. Keightley and M. Pickering (2012) *The Mnemonic Imagination: Remembering as Creative Practice* (Basingstoke: Palgrave Macmillan).

S. Kirchgaessner (2018) 'Italy's Salvini warns EU to "defend its border" against migrants', *Guardian* (20 June), https://www.theguardian.com/world/2018/jun/20/italys-salvini-warns-eu-to-defend-its-border-against-migrants. Accessed 3 November 2018.

U. Klinger and J. Svensson (2014) 'The Emergence of Network Media Logic in Political Communication: A Theoretical Approach', *New Media & Society*, 17:8, pp. 1241–1257.

M. Kyriakidou (2015) 'Media Witnessing: Exploring the Audience of Distant Suffering', *Media, Culture & Society*, 37:2, pp. 215–231.

H. Lambert and T. Farrell (2010) 'The Changing Character of Armed Conflict and the Implications for Refugee Protection Jurisprudence', *International Journal of Refugee Law*, 22:2, pp. 237–273.

A. Lele (2014) 'Asymmetric Warfare: A State vs Non-State Conflict', *OASIS*, 20, pp. 97–111.

K. Leurs (2017) 'Communication Rights from the Margins: Politicising Young Refugees' Smartphone Pocket Archives', *International Communication Gazette*, 79:6–7, pp. 674–698.

K. Leurs and S. Ponzanesi (2018) 'Connected Migrants: Encapsulation and Cosmopolitanisation', *Popular Communication*, 16:1, pp. 4–20.

G. Loescher (2001) *The UNHCR and World Politics: A Perilous Path* (Oxford: Oxford University Press).

A. Lorde (1984) *Sister Outsider: Essays and Speeches* (Berkeley, CA: Ten Speed Press).

D. Madison (2005) *Critical Ethnography: Methods, Ethics, and Performance* (London: SAGE).

B. Martill (2017) 'Britain has lost a role, and failed to find an empire', *UCL European Institute* (17 January), https://www.ucl.ac.uk/european-institute/news/2017/jan/britain-has-lost-role-and-failed-find-empire. Accessed 10 November 2018.

A. Mbembe (2015) 'Decolonising knowledge and the question of the archive', *Wits University*, https://wiser.wits.ac.za/system/files/Achille%20Mbembe%20-%20Decolonizing%20Knowledge%20and%20the%20Question%20of%20the%20Archive.pdf. Accessed 10 November 2018.

M. McCall (2000) 'Performance Ethnography: A Brief History and Some Advice', in N. Denzin and Y. Lincoln (eds), *Handbook of Qualitative Research* (Thousand Oaks, CA: SAGE), pp. 421–433.

G. McFadyen (2016) 'The Language of Labelling and the Politics of Hostipitality in the British Asylum System', *British Journal of Politics and International Relations*, 18:3, pp. 599–617.

G. McLaughlin (2016) *The War Correspondent* (London: Pluto Press).

C. Mead (2013) *War Play: Video Games and the Future of Armed Conflict* (Boston, MA: Houghton Mifflin Harcourt).

A. Meek (2010) *Trauma and Media: Theories, Histories and Images* (Abingdon: Routledge).

C. Meijer and T. Groot Kormelink (2015) 'Checking, Sharing, Clicking and Linking: Changing Patterns of Use Between 2004 and 2014', *Digital Journalism*, 3:5, pp. 664–679.

M. Mellino (2012) 'De-Provincializing Italy: Notes on Race, Racialization, and Italy's Coloniality', in C. Lombardi-Diop and C. Romeo (eds), *Postcolonial Italy: Challenging National Homogeneity* (Cham, Switzerland: Springer Publishing), pp. 83–99.

J. Mermin (1997) 'Television News and American Intervention in Somalia: The Myth of a Media-Driven Foreign Policy', *Political Science Quarterly*, 112:3, pp. 385–403.

Il Messagero (2017) 'Gentiloni: "Soldati in Niger per sconfiggere il traffico di essere umani e il terrorismo"', *Il Messagero* (24 December), https://www.ilmessaggero.it/primopiano/politica/gentiloni_soldati_niger_sconfiggere_traffico_essere_umani_terrorismo-3447765.html. Accessed 10 November 2018.

S. Mezzadra and B. Nielson (2013) *Border as Method, or, The Multiplication of Labour* (Durham, NC: Duke University Press).

N. Mirzoeff (2012) *Watching Babylon: The War in Iraq and Global Visual Culture* (London: Routledge).

A. Mitra (2017) 'The MacAulay speech that never was', *The Wire India* (19 February), https://thewire.in/history/macaulays-speech-never-delivered. Accessed 10 November 2018.

Bibliography

M. Mortensen, S. Allan and C. Peters (2017) 'The Iconic Image in a Digital Age', *Nordicom Review*, 38 s2, pp. 71–86.

J. W. Müller (2016) *What is Populism?* (London: Penguin Books).

J. Muthyala (2006) *Reworlding America: Myth, History and Narrative* (Athens, OH: Ohio University Press).

T. Nail (2016) 'A Tale of Two Crises: Migration and Terrorism after the Paris Attacks', *Studies in Ethnicities and Nationalism*, 16:1, pp. 158–167.

C. Neumayer (2016) 'Nationalist and Anti-Fascist Movements in Social Media', in A. Bruns, G. Enli, E. Skoverbø E, et al. (eds), *The Routledge Companion to Social Media and Politics* (New York: Routledge), pp. 296–307.

E. Newman (2004) 'The "New Wars" Debate: A Historical Perspective is Needed', *Security Dialogue*, 35:2, pp. 173–189.

A. A. Nohrstedt and R. Ottosen (2014) *New Wars, New Media and New War Journalism: Professional and Legal Challenges in Conflict Reporting* (Göteborg, Nordicom).

M. Norfolk, 2016 'Apartheid of Asylum Seekers on British Streets', *The Times* (20 January), https://www.thetimes.co.uk/article/apartheid-of-the-asylum-seekers-on-british-streets-hl98brdx2v2. Accessed 30 September 2016.

P. Noto and S. Pesce (2018) *The Politics of Ephemeral Digital Media* (New York: Routledge).

L. De Noronha (2018) 'Race, class and Brexit: thinking from detention', Verso Books (9 March), https://www.versobooks.com/blogs/3675-race-class-and-brexit-thinking-from-detention. Accessed 1 August 2018.

E. Ochs and L. Capps (2001) *Living Narrative: Creating Lives in Everyday Storytelling* (Cambridge, MA: Harvard University Press).

Office for National Statistics (2013) '2011 Census: Country of birth (expanded), regions in England and Wales', *Office for National Statistics* (26 March), http://www.ons.gov.uk/ons/rel/census/2011-census/quick-statistics-for-england-and-wales-on-national-identity-passports-held-and-country-of-birth/rft-qs213ew.xls. Accessed 10 September 2018.

F. Ogundimu and J. Fair (1997) 'Before "Hope Was Restored": News Media Portrayals of Somalia Prior to the U.S. Intervention', *Northeast African Studies New Series*, 4:2, pp. 19–41.

F. Oliveri (2016) 'Where are Our Sons? Tunisian Families and the Re-Politicization of Deadly Migration Across the Mediterranean Sea', in L. Mannik (ed.), *Migration by Boat: Discourses of Trauma, Exclusion, and Survival* (New York: Berghahn Books), pp. 154–177.

F. Oliveri (2017) '"Open the Border": Migrant Struggles for Freedom of Movement in the Crisis of the Euro-Mediterranean Border Regime', in G. David (ed.), *Nous sommes ici* (Palermo: Glifo Edizioni), pp. 131–135.

M. Omi and H. Winant (1994) *Racial Formation in the United States, from the 1960s to the 1990s* (New York and London: Routledge).

A. Ophir (2010) 'The Politics of Catastrophization: Emergency and Exception', in D. Fassin and M. Pandolfi (eds), *Contemporary States of Emergency: The*

Politics of Military and Humanitarian Interventions (New York: Zone Books), pp. 59–88.
B. Orend (2006) *The Morality of War* (Toronto: Broadview Press).
E. Paoletti (2010) 'Power Relations and International Migration: The Case of Italy and Libya', *Political Studies*, 59:2, pp. 269–289.
D. Patrikarakos (2017) *War in 140 Characters: How Social Media is Reshaping Conflict in the Twenty-First Century* (New York: Basic Books).
I. Pentina and M. Tarafdar (2014) 'From "Information" to "Knowing": Exploring the Role of Social Media in Contemporary News Consumption', *Computers in Human Behaviour*, 35 (June), pp. 211–223.
K. Perry (2007) 'Sharing Stories, Linking Lives: Literacy Practices Among Sudanese Refugees', in V. Purcell-Gates (ed.), *Cultural Practices of Literacy: Case Studies of Language, Literacy, Social Practice, and Power* (Mahwah, NJ: Lawrence Erlbaum), pp. 57–84.
W. Phillips and R. Milner (2017) *The Ambivalent Internet* (Cambridge: Polity Press).
G. Philo, E. Briant and P. Donald (2013) *Bad News for Refugees* (London: Pluto Press).
G. Philo, L. Hilsum, L. Beattie and R. Holliman (1998) 'The Media and the Rwanda Crisis: Effects on Audiences and Public Policy', in J.N. Pieterse (ed.), *World Orders in the Making: Humanitarian Intervention and Beyond* (Basingstoke: Palgrave Macmillan), pp. 211–229.
Il Post (2018) 'La storia dei 67 migranti soccorsi dalla Vos Thalassa, dall'inizio' (11 July), https://www.ilpost.it/2018/07/11/storia-migranti-vos-thalassa-diciotti-salvini. Accessed 10 November 2018.
Presidio Permanente No Borders Ventimiglia, https://www.facebook.com/pages/category/Community/Presidio-Permanente-No-Borders-Ventimiglia-782827925168723/. Accessed 1 November 2018.
'Raising £1,000 to welcome Syrian families across West Kent by supplying essentials to assist their new start in life', *JustGiving* (2017), https://www.justgiving.com/crowdfunding/familycampingevent. Accessed 10 September 2017.
Refugee Council 2018 'The facts about asylum' https://www.refugeecouncil.org.uk/policy_research/the_truth_about_asylum/facts_about_asylum_-_page_6. Accessed 12 November 2018.
Refugee Council 2018 https://en-gb.facebook.com/pages/category/Community/Refugees-Not-Welcome-1004579652932069/. Accessed 10 October 2018.
Refugees at Home https://en-gb.facebook.com/refugeesathome/. Accessed 10 November 2018.
M. Renzi (2017) *Avanti. Perché l'Italia non si ferma* (Milan: Feltrinelli).
Right to Remain (2017) 'Politics before protection: the story of Eritrean asylum seekers in the UK', *Right to Remain* (29 January), https://righttoremain.org.uk/

politics-before-protection-the-story-of-eritrean-asylum-seekers-in-the-uk/. Accessed 13 November 2018.

A. Roberts (1993) 'Humanitarian War: Military Intervention and Human Rights', *International Affairs*, 69:3, pp. 429–449.

A. Roberts (1999) 'NATO's "Humanitarian War" over Kosovo', *Survival*, 41:3 (Autumn), pp. 102–123.

K. Robins (1993) 'The War, the Screen, the Crazy Dog and Poor Mankind', *Media Culture & Society*, 15:2, pp. 321–327.

P. Robinson (2002) *The CNN effect: The Myth of News, Foreign Policy and Intervention* (New York: Routledge).

L. Romano (2018) 'Vos Thalassa, migranti in rivolta sulla nave: "L'equipaggio rischiava la vita"', *Il Giornale* (10 July), http://www.ilgiornale.it/news/cronache/vos-thalassa-toninelli-bordo-migranti-facinorosi-lequipaggio-1551320.html. Accessed 10 September 2018.

S. Romanò (2015) 'Milano al collasso, il sindaco Pisapia annuncia: "Basta nuovi profughi"', *Leggo* (15 June), https://www.leggo.it/news/milano/milano_profughi_sindaco_pisapia-1093149.html. Accessed 1 October 2018.

R. Rorty (1989) *Contingency, Irony, and Solidarity* (Cambridge: Cambridge University Press).

E. Said (1978) *Orientalism* (London: Penguin).

J. Saldaña (2005) *Ethnodrama: An Anthology of Reality Theatre* (Walnut Creek, CA: AltaMira Press).

M. Salvini (2018) 'Caso Aquarius. Salvini: sono stufo di vedere bambini morti nel Mediterraneo', *RAI News* (13 June), http://www.rainews.it/dl/rainews/media/caso-aquarius-salvini-sono-stufo-di-vedere-bambini-morti-nel-mediterraneo-f1dc00ec-2583-4692-b47a-a68f0bocefe9.html. Accessed 1 October 2018.

F. Sarzanini (2018) 'Migranti, scontro Italia-Malta. Salvini: "Porti chiusi all'Aquarius" Conte: "Noi lasciati soli"', *Corriere* (11 June), https://roma.corriere.it/notizie/cronaca/18_giugno_11/migranti-salvini-la-aquarius-non-potra-approdare-un-porto-italiano-28e19a16-6cb2-11e8-8fe1-92e098249b61.shtml. Accessed 10 November 2018.

A. Sayad (1992) *L'Immigration, ou les paradoxes de l'altérité* (Brussels: De Boeck).

K. Schroder (2015) 'News Media Old and New, Fluctuating Audiences, News Repertoires and Locations of Consumption', *Journalism Studies*, 16:1, pp. 60–78.

P. Seib (2008) *The Aljazeera Effect: How the New Global Media are Reshaping World Politics* (Dulles: Potamac Books).

E. Siapera, M. Boudourides, S. Lenis, J. Suiter (2018) 'Refugees and Network Publics on Twitter: Networked Framing, Affect, and Capture', *Social Media + Society* (January–March), pp. 1–21.

P. Slovic, D. Västfjäll, A. Erlandsson and R. Gregory (2017) 'Iconic Photographs and the Ebb and Flow of Empathic Response to Humanitarian Disasters', *PNAS*, 114:4, pp. 640–644.

G. Spivak (1992) 'Asked to Talk about Myself', *Third Text*, 6:19, pp. 9–18.

G. Spivak (2006) *In Other Worlds: Essays in Cultural Politics* (Abingdon: Routledge).

R. Stahl (2010) *Militainment, Inc.: War, Media, and Popular Culture* (London: Routledge).

E. Steinhilper and R. J. Gruijters (2018) 'A Contested Crisis: Policy Narratives and Empirical Evidence on Border Deaths in the Mediterranean', *Sociology*, 52:3 pp. 515–533.

Stop Invasione https://www.facebook.com/StopInvasioneClandestina/. Accessed 1 September 2018.

J. Stumpf (2006) 'The Crimmigration Crisis: Immigrants, Crime and Sovereign Power', *American University Law Review*, 56:2, pp. 368–419.

M. Szczepanik (2016) 'The "Good" and "Bad" Refugees? Imagined Refugeehood(s) in the Media Coverage of the Migration Crisis', *Journal of Identity & Migration Studies*, 10:2, pp. 23–33.

Y. Theocharis and E. Quintelier (2016) 'Stimulating Citizenship or Expanding Entertainment? The Effect of Facebook on Adolescent Participation', *New Media & Society*, 18:5, pp. 817–836.

A. Thompson (ed.) (2007) *The Media and the Rwanda Genocide* (London: Pluto Press).

D. K. Thussu (2003) 'Live TV and Bloodless Deaths: War, Infotainment and 24/7 news', in D.K. Thussu and D. Freedman (eds), *War and the Media: Reporting Conflict 24/7* (London: SAGE), pp. 117–132.

D. K. Thussu (2008) *News as Entertainment: The Rise of Global Infotainment* (London: SAGE).

M. Todorova (2009) *Imagining the Balkans* (Oxford: Oxford University Press).

L. Tondo and P. Messina (2018) 'Interpol circulates list of suspected Isis fighters believed to be in Italy', *Guardian* (31 January), https://www.theguardian.com/world/2018/jan/31/interpol-circulates-list-of-suspected-isis-fighters-believed-to-be-in-italy. Accessed 5 November 2018.

A. Triulzi (2012) 'Hidden Faces, Hidden Histories: Contrasting Voices of Postcolonial Italy', in C. Lombardi-Diop and C. Romeo (eds), *Postcolonial Italy: Challenging National Homogeneity* (Cham, Switzerland: Springer Publishing), pp. 103–113.

B. Turner and C. Rojek (2001) *Society and Culture: Principles of Solidarity and Scarcity* (London: SAGE).

UNHCR (1979) *Handbook and Guidelines on Procedures and Criteria for Determining Refugee Status under the 1951 Convention and the 1967 Protocol Relating to the Status of Refugees* (Geneva: UNHCR).

UNHCR (2017) *Mid-Year Trends 2016* (Geneva: UNHCR).

UNHCR (2018) *Global Trends: Forced Displacement in 2017* (Geneva: UNHCR).

UN News (2015) 'UN rights chief urges UK to curb tabloid hate speech, end "decades of abuse" targeting migrants', *UN News* (24 April), https://news.un.org/en/story/2015/04/496892-un-rights-chief-urges-uk-curb-tabloid-hate-speech-end-decades-abuse-targeting. Accessed 15 September 2018.

N. Vaughan-Williams (2015) *Europe's Border Crisis: Biopolitical Security and Beyond* (Oxford: Oxford University Press).

N. Vaughan-Williams (2018) '"We Are Not Animals!" Humanitarian Border Security and Zoopolitical Spaces in Europe', *Political Geography*, 45, pp. 1–10.

M. Vimalassery, J.H. Pegues and A. Goldstein (2017) 'Colonial Unknowing and Relations of Study', *Theory & Event*, 20:4, pp. 1042–1054.

I. Wallerstein (2004) *World-Systems Analysis: An Introduction* (Durham, NC: Duke University Press).

M. Walzer (1997) *Just and Unjust Wars: A Moral Argument with Historical Illustrations* (New York: Basic Books).

G. Wekker (2016) *White Innocence: Paradoxes of Colonialism and Race* (Durham, NC: Duke University Press).

West Midlands Solidarity with Refugees (2018) https://www.facebook.com/groups/575611285910286/. Accessed 13 November 2018.

O. Westlund and M.A. Fardigh (2015) 'Accessing the News in an Age of Mobile Media: Tracing Displacing and Complementary Effects of Mobile News on Newspapers and Online News', *Mobile Media and Communication*, 3:1, pp. 53–74.

N. Wheeler (2000) *Saving Strangers: Humanitarian Intervention in International Society* (Oxford: Oxford University Press).

M. Wood, J. Corbett and M. Flinders (2016) 'Just Like Us: Everyday Celebrity Politicians and the Pursuit of Popularity in an Age of Anti-Politics', *The British Journal of Politics and International Relations*, 18:3, pp. 581–598.

N. Yuval-Davis, G. Wemyss and K. Cassidy (2017) 'Everyday Bordering, Belonging and the Reorientation of British Immigration Legislation', *Sociology*, 25:2, pp. 228–244.

N. Yuval-Davis, G. Wemyss and K. Cassidy (2019) *Bordering* (Cambridge: Polity).

B. Zelizer (2011) 'Photography, Journalism and Trauma', in B. Zelizer and S. Allen (eds), *Journalism after September 11th* (Abingdon: Routledge), pp. 55–75.

Index

Index

Index